The **Primary Comprehension Toolkit** Language and Lessons for Active Literacy

Stephanie Harvey & Anne Goudvis

Keep Reading!

a sourcebook of short text

Copyright ©2008 by Stephanie Harvey and Anne Goudvis
All rights reserved.

The authors and publisher wish to thank those who have generously given permission to reprint borrowed materials.

Library of Congress Catalog-in-Publication Data
CIP data on file with the Library of Congress

Keep Reading! A Source Book of Short Text
ISBN-13: 978-0-325-02155-3
ISBN-10: 0-325-02155-4

Primary Comprehension Toolkit: Language and Lessons for Active Literacy
ISBN-13: 978-0-325-00997-1
ISBN-10: 0-325-00997-X

Printed in the United States of America on acid-free paper

DEDICATED TO TEACHERS™

*first*hand
An imprint of Heinemann
361 Hanover Street
Portsmouth, NH 03801
firsthand.heinemann.com
Offices and agents throughout the world

13   ML   5

Contents

Keep Reading!

a sourcebook of short text

Introduction

As we reiterate throughout the *Toolkit*: Text matters—a lot! When we are teaching comprehension strategies to primary kids, we need lots and lots of great, engaging text—books, magazines, posters, and more. In this volume, we have collected two categories of nonfiction text and put together a bibliography of text and resources for both children and teachers.

Lesson Text

Many of the *Toolkit* lessons are built around compelling exemplary text that we've tested in classrooms across the country and can guarantee students find engaging. These include six *TIME For Kids Big Picture Edition* articles and *The National Geographic Young Explorer* magazine "Fly With a Butterfly." Note that not all of the lesson text is included in *Keep Reading*. For example, some of the lessons are built on picture books which you may find in your classroom or school library; if not, consider purchasing the optional *Primary Toolkit Trade Book Pack*.

Nonfiction Short Text

When you introduce kids to the *Toolkit* strategies, it's important that you use text that naturally appeals to them and will almost certainly capture their attention. In addition to the lesson text, *Keep Reading* includes an amazing variety of 39 additional informational articles that are not used in the lessons. The articles are geared to kindergarten, first, and second grade learners. Packed with illustrations, photographs, maps, charts, and the like, these articles cover a range of engaging topics for young kids including nature, animals, weather, city and country life, families, art, sports, and more.

Note that we've organized the *Nonfiction Short Text* articles thematically and by reading challenge. (See page 49.) Nearly every thematic grouping includes texts that are easy to read and others that offer a greater challenge. Some of the articles are wordless, offering a wonderful opportunity for our earliest readers to create meaning by viewing the images. Others feature a brief label or a few simple sentences for those readers who are just beginning to crack the code. Still other articles combine rich, descriptive text with detailed photos to support more developed readers to learn information and come up with big ideas. And don't forget—if you want these articles in full color, they can be downloaded from the *Toolkit* DVD-ROM.

The articles are multi-functional. They offer a good alternative to the lesson text we include in the *Toolkit* and you can use them to provide instruction in any of the *Toolkit* lessons. They are also useful for additional comprehension instruction and practice in needs-based, flexible, guided reading groups. And most importantly, kids can choose them for independent reading and for fun!

The teachers with whom we work immediately recognize the value of short nonfiction text. They always want to know where they can get their hands on some. We are delighted to offer a great selection of captivating articles right here in *Keep Reading*, our source book of short text.

Bibliography

The bibliography at the end of this source book includes a list of social studies and science trade books of particular interest to primary grade kids, a selection of magazines and websites for primary teachers and readers, a list of professional books that have enhanced our understanding of reading comprehension practice and nonfiction literacy, and an array of books that celebrate the joy of reading.

TIME FOR KIDS

Whales Swim South

Taking a Trip

Each fall, snow geese and many other animals head for their winter homes.

VOL. 2 • NO. 4 THEME

www.timeforkids.com   AOL Keyword: TFK

A Ride in the Sky

With the sound of honks and the flapping of wings, the geese are off. They are on their way to warm-weather homes. The trip that geese and other animals take each season is called **migration**.

Geese live up north in the summer. They leave in the fall.

Flocks of geese travel in a V shape. The birds in the back can rest.

Geese settle in a warm winter home. They fly back north in the spring.

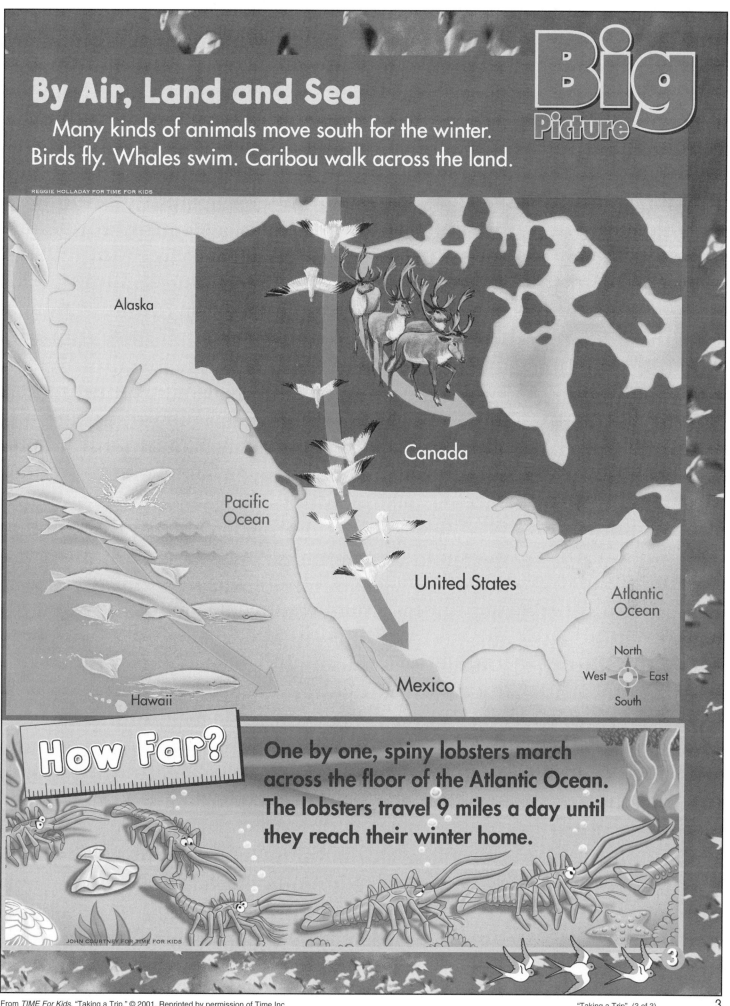

By Air, Land and Sea

Many kinds of animals move south for the winter.
Birds fly. Whales swim. Caribou walk across the land.

REGGIE HOLLADAY FOR TIME FOR KIDS

Alaska

Canada

Pacific
Ocean

United States

Atlantic
Ocean

North

West — East

South

Hawaii

Mexico

How Far?

One by one, spiny lobsters march
across the floor of the Atlantic Ocean.
The lobsters travel 9 miles a day until
they reach their winter home.

JOHN COURTNEY FOR TIME FOR KIDS

Notes

Ideas about using this TFK poster for additional comprehension lessons

TIME FOR KIDS

Can You Spot the Spider?

Spiders!

Spiders have sneaky ways of getting their meals.

VOL. 3 • NO. 4 THEME

www.timeforkids.com   AOL Keyword: TFK

Feed Me!

When a spider is hungry, watch out! Spiders have many amazing ways to trap insects. Some can even catch a fish!

Spiders sneak up.

The trapdoor spider builds a hole with a door. When an insect walks by, out pops the spider!

Spiders go fishing.

The water spider floats underwater in a bubble web. It sticks out its legs to fish. Then it pulls in its meal.

Spiders jump.

The jumping spider spots an insect. It flies through the air. Pounce! It has its dinner.

2

JAMES P. ROWAN—DRK PHOTO. BORDER: CHRISTOPHER A. RECORD—THE CHARLOTTE OBSERVER/AP

Spiders hide.

Can you see the spider on the flower? Many insects can't. The crab spider blends in. It surprises insects that drop by. Then it eats them!

How Big?

Some spiders work in groups to catch food. They weave webs together. The webs are so big they can cover a tree. The giant web can trap prey that is 10 times bigger than the spider!

3

Parts of a Spider

Study the parts of a spider's body. Then answer the questions below.
Fill in the bubbles next to the right answers.

front body part

back body part

spinnerets

8 eyes

legs

fangs

Think Big!

How do spiders use webs to catch food?

1. How many legs does a spider have?
   ○ 4   ○ 7   ○ 8

2. The back and front body parts are different. The back of this spider is
   ○ bigger   ○ smaller   ○ the same size

3. A spider has fangs. What else is on the same body part?
   ○ nose   ○ ears   ○ eyes

4. A spider uses spinnerets to spin silk for webs. Spinnerets are on the
   ○ front body part   ○ back body part   ○ legs

Parents: Even though spiders have many eyes, they can't see well. Have your child close his or her eyes. Discuss how you can use your other senses to tell what is near.

TIME FOR KIDS THE BIG PICTURE (ISSN 1528-6584) is published 15 times a year biweekly from September to May except during Thanksgiving, Christmas and Easter/Passover for the classroom rate of $3.75 per student (minimum order: 10 copies) by Time Inc. Principal Office: Time & Life Building, 1271 Avenue of the Americas, New York, NY 10020-1393. Ann Moore, Chairman, CEO; Richard Atkinson, Treasurer; Robert E. McCarthy, Secretary. Periodical postage paid at New York, NY, and at additional mailing offices. © 2002 Time Inc. All rights reserved. Reproduction in whole or in part without written permission is prohibited. TIME FOR KIDS is a registered trademark of Time Inc. Subscriber: If the postal authorities alert us that your magazine is undeliverable, we have no further obligation unless we receive a corrected address within two years. POSTMASTER: Send address changes to TIME FOR KIDS, P.O. Box 30609, Tampa, FL 33630-0609. Subscription queries: 1-800-950-5966. Mailing list: We make a portion of our mailing list available to reputable firms. If you prefer that we not include your name, please call or write us at P.O. Box 60001, Tampa, FL 33630, or send us an e-mail at privacy@timecustomersvc.com.

④   COVER PHOTO: JOE MCDONALD—DRK PHOTO; INSET: JOHN GERLACH—ANIMALS ANIMALS

TIME FOR KIDS

Bugs in Eggs

LADYBUGS GROW UP

These little insects
start in eggs.
Then they change
and change.
Find out how!

THEME: LIFE CYCLES

www.timeforkids.com

A Ladybug's Life

The life cycle of a ladybug begins in the spring. A ladybug passes through three stages. Then it becomes an adult beetle.

1 Egg

A female ladybug finds a leaf. It lays hundreds of eggs. The tiny oval eggs stay close together.

JEROME WEXLER—VISUALS UNLIMITED

2 Larva

After a few days, the eggs hatch. Out come little bugs that look like alligators. Each is called a larva. It eats many aphids and gets big.

ROBERT PICKETT—PAPILIO/ALAMY

SCOTT CAMAZINE

From *TIME For Kids*, "Ladybugs Grow Up," © 2005. Reprinted by permission of Time Inc.

3 Pupa

The larva sheds its skin a few times over the next two to three weeks. A new, hard skin grows, and the ladybug turns into a pupa.

STEPHEN DALTON—NHPA

4 Adult

A soft, wet ladybug comes out of the pupa after about a week. Its outer wings get hard. Its color gets bright. The ladybug is all grown!

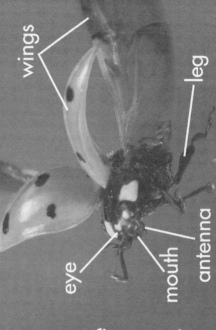

wings

leg

antenna

mouth

eye

ALAMY. BACKGROUND PHOTO: BRUCE BURKHARDT—CORBIS

Science Scoop

Look at a ladybug's body. Like all insects, a ladybug has three main body parts and six legs. It has two hard outside wings that protect the thin inside wings.

TIME FOR KIDS

Name: _____

Meet a Mammal

Look at the chart to learn a deer's life cycle.

Think Big!

In what ways do you think all animals change as they grow up?

ANNE REAS FOR TIME FOR KIDS

A Deer Grows Up

Baby	Youth	Adult

• A deer is born live. • One, two or three babies are born. • Babies drink milk from their mothers.	• Fawns learn to run. • Fawns have red-brown fur with spots. • A fawn stays with its mom for a year.	• Adults are active at night. • Adult deer fur turns gray-brown in winter. • Males have antlers.

Choose a word from the word box to complete each sentence.

1. An _____ male deer has antlers.

2. A _____ is born live.

3. A _____ learns to run at a few weeks old.

Word Box
baby   youth   adult

 Parents: Discuss your child's growth. Look at baby and toddler photos to point out the ways your child has changed. Discuss changes that lie ahead.

④

COVER: YVES LANCEAU—NHPA; INSET: NIGEL CATTLIN—ALAMY

From *TIME For Kids*, "Ladybugs Grow Up," © 2005. Reprinted by permission of Time Inc.

THE BIG PICTURE • WINTER 2002 • WOMEN'S HISTORY MONTH

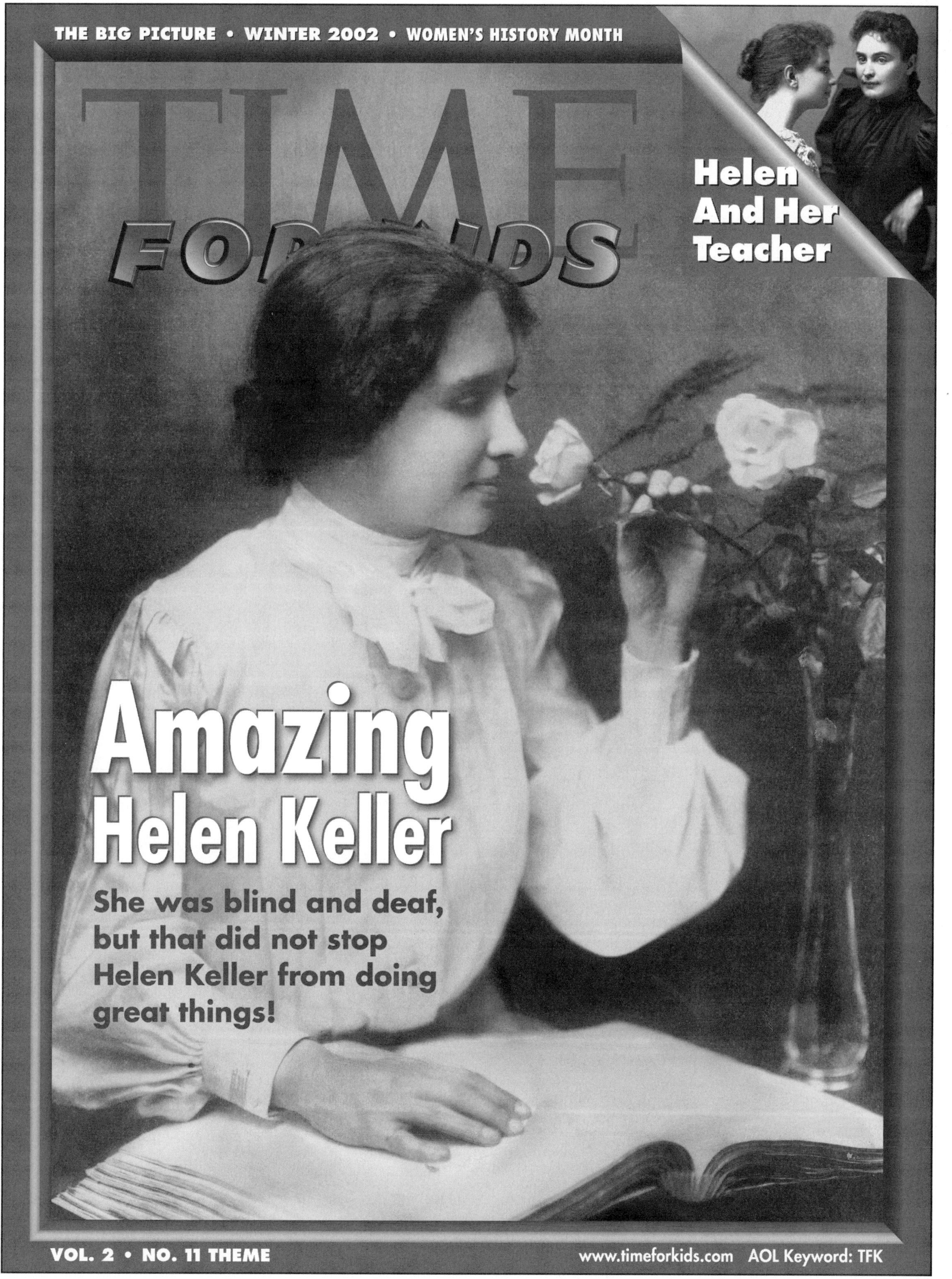

TIME FOR KIDS

Helen And Her Teacher

Amazing Helen Keller

She was blind and deaf, but that did not stop Helen Keller from doing great things!

VOL. 2 • NO. 11 THEME

www.timeforkids.com AOL Keyword: TFK

An Amazing Life

Helen Keller was born more than 120 years ago. She became blind and deaf when she was just a baby. A special teacher helped her learn to read and speak. Helen Keller did not let anything stand in her way!

Age 7

Helen had no way to speak until she was 7. Then she began to learn sign language.

Age 19

Annie Sullivan taught Helen to spell words with her hands. She even went to college with Helen.

Age 39

Helen loved horseback riding. She believed that blind and deaf people could do almost anything.

2

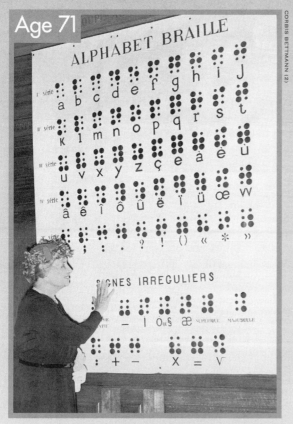

Age 71

ALPHABET BRAILLE

SIGNES IRREGULIERS

She helped other blind and deaf people learn to read. Here she is with an alphabet for the blind.

Age 80

Helen became famous. She met President John F. Kennedy and 11 other Presidents!

How Many?

Helen Keller's first book was called *The Story of My Life*. People around the world have read it. The book has been printed in more than 50 languages!

RON ZALME FOR TIME FOR KIDS; COUNTERS: RITA LASCARO FOR TIME FOR KIDS

 TIME FOR KIDS THE BIG PICTURE

3

Talking with Your Hands

People who are deaf use their hands to speak. Look at the American Sign Language alphabet. Use it to figure out the three words below. Write a word on each line.

Think Big!

Name the five senses. Which ones did Helen Keller use?

1. _____

2. _____

3. _____

Bonus: Use your hands to say your name in sign language.

 Now Hear This! Hear Big Picture read aloud. Go to **www.timeforkids.com/bigpic**

TIME FOR KIDS THE BIG PICTURE (ISSN 1528-6584) is published 15 times a year biweekly from September to May except during Thanksgiving, Christmas and Easter/Passover for the classroom rate of $3.50 per student (minimum order: 10 copies) by Time Inc. Principal Office: Time & Life Building, 1271 Avenue of the Americas, New York, NY 10020- 1393. Don Logan, Chairman, CEO; Richard Atkinson, Treasurer; Robert E. McCarthy, Secretary. Periodical postage paid at New York, NY, and at additional mailing offices. © 2002 Time Inc. All rights reserved. Reproduction in whole or in part without written permission is prohibited. TIME FOR KIDS is a registered trademark of Time Inc. Subscriber: If the postal authorities alert us that your magazine is undeliverable, we have no further obligation unless we receive a corrected address within two years. POSTMASTER: Send address changes to TIME FOR KIDS, P.O. Box 30609, Tampa, FL 33630-0609. Subscription queries: 1-800-950-5966. Mailing list: We make a portion of our mailing list available to reputable firms. If you prefer that we not include your name, please call or write us at P.O. Box 60001, Tampa, FL 33630, or send us an e-mail at privacy@timecustomersvc.com.

COVER PHOTO: CORBIS BETTMANN: HAND COLORING BY JOAN MENSCHENFREUND FOR TFK; INSET: CORBIS BETTMANN

4

RITA LASCARO FOR TIME FOR KIDS

TIME FOR KIDS

Mexico's **History**

A Visit to Mexico

This girl is dressed up for a festival.
What else could you see on a trip to Mexico?

Our Neighbor

Mexico is our neighbor. It is the sunny country south of the United States. Mexico is famous for its music, art, food, native people and more!

United States

Mexico

Mexico City★

Mexico has many farms. The United States gets many fresh fruits and vegetables from Mexico.

Mexico has big cities. The capital is City. It is one of the biggest cities in world! Look at the Mexican flag fly

Mexico has pyramids. They were made by people who lived there thousands of years ago.

2

JEAN WISENBAUGH FOR TIME FOR KIDS

North
West—East
South

LARRY DALE GORDON—GETTY IMAGES

PICTURE FINDERS LTD.—ESTOCK PHOTO

Mexico
the
ng there.

Mexico has colorful festivals and holidays. People dress up, dance and sing for Cinco de Mayo (SINK-oh day MY-oh).

How Much?

||||| |||||

People in Mexico speak Spanish. They use pesos for money. Ten pesos are about the same as one U.S. dollar.

DAVE KLUG FOR TIME FOR KIDS

③

Notes

Ideas about using this TFK poster for additional comprehension lessons

_____

_____

_____

_____

_____

_____

_____

_____

_____

_____

_____

_____

TIME FOR KIDS

Frogs of All Sizes

A colorful toucan

Welcome to the Rain Forest

The rain forest is one of the most colorful habitats in the world. From the ground to the treetops, it is bursting with living things.

The Forest Roof

It is green, wet and hot. It is full of trees and full of life. The busiest layer of the rain forest is called the **canopy**. Meet some canopy animals.

GEORGE GRALL—GETTY IMAGES

Some animals stand out.

The color of these frogs sends a warning. It says, "Watch out!" The frogs have poison.

MICHAEL & PATRICIA FOGDEN—MINDEN PICTURES

Some animals hang around.

Sloths spend hours hanging from trees. Look at the baby clinging to its mom.

MICHAEL J. DOOLITTLE; FLOWER BORDER: MICHAEL & PATRICIA FOGDEN—MINDEN PICTURES

MICHAEL & PATRICIA FOGDEN—MINDEN PICTURES

Some animals come out at night.

This insect is a horned katydid. Its spikes scare off enemies. It chirps songs each night.

2

How Small?

One kind of monkey is so tiny that it can fit in a teacup! It lives in the Amazon in South America. The Amazon is the largest rain forest. It has at least 80 kinds of monkeys.

People can explore the canopy.
Scientists study the canopy. Visitors enjoy its beauty. Walking on bridges high above the ground is one way to explore.

3

Name:

Look at the Layers

Study the picture. It shows the parts of a rain forest.

Think
Big!
Why should we protect rain forests?

Emergents

Canopy

Understory

Forest Floor

Draw a line to match each fact with the name of the rain forest layer.

1. Birds fly from treetop to treetop here.

2. This layer makes a forest roof.

3. Jaguars live on this bottom layer.

4. This shady layer has many leafy plants.

Forest Floor

Understory

Canopy

Emergents

BARBARA SPURLL FOR TIME FOR KIDS

Parents: **Help your child learn more from the picture above. Discuss how many colors there are and how many animals you can name.**

TIME FOR KIDS THE BIG PICTURE (ISSN 1528-6584) is published 15 times a year biweekly from September to May except school holidays for the classroom rate of $3.75 per student (minimum order: 10 copies) by Time Inc. Principal Office: Time & Life Building, 1271 Avenue of the Americas, New York, NY 10020-1393. Ann S. Moore, Chairman, CEO; Richard Atkinson, Treasurer; Robert E. McCarthy, Secretary. Periodical postage paid at New York, NY, and at additional mailing offices. © 2003 Time Inc. All rights reserved. Reproduction in whole or in part without written permission is prohibited. TIME FOR KIDS is a registered trademark of Time Inc. Subscriber: If the postal authorities alert us that your magazine is undeliverable, we have no further obligation unless we receive a corrected address within two years. POSTMASTER: Send address changes to TIME FOR KIDS, P.O. Box 30609, Tampa, FL 33630-0609. Subscription queries: 1-800-950-5966. Mailing list: We make a portion of our mailing list available to reputable firms. If you prefer that we not include your name, please call or write us at P.O. Box 60001, Tampa, FL 33630, or send us an e-mail at privacy@timecustomersvc.com.

4

COVER PHOTO: KEVIN SCHAFER—CORBIS; INSET: T. DAVIS—PHOTORESEARCHERS

NATIONAL GEOGRAPHIC
Young Explorer!

Fly With a Butterfly ₂

How Seeds Spread 16

© SUPERSTOCK / AGE PHOTOSTOCK

2

A Butterfly Is Born

Spring is here.
So are butterflies.

3

A **butterfly** sits on a plant.
She lays an **egg**.

butterfly

4

A butterfly egg is small.
It will hatch soon.
A **caterpillar** will come out.

egg

5

The caterpillar is hungry.
It eats the plant.
The caterpillar grows.

caterpillar

The caterpillar changes.
It hangs from a plant.
It makes a **chrysalis**.

caterpillar

chrysalis

7

The caterpillar stays in the chrysalis. It turns into a **pupa**.

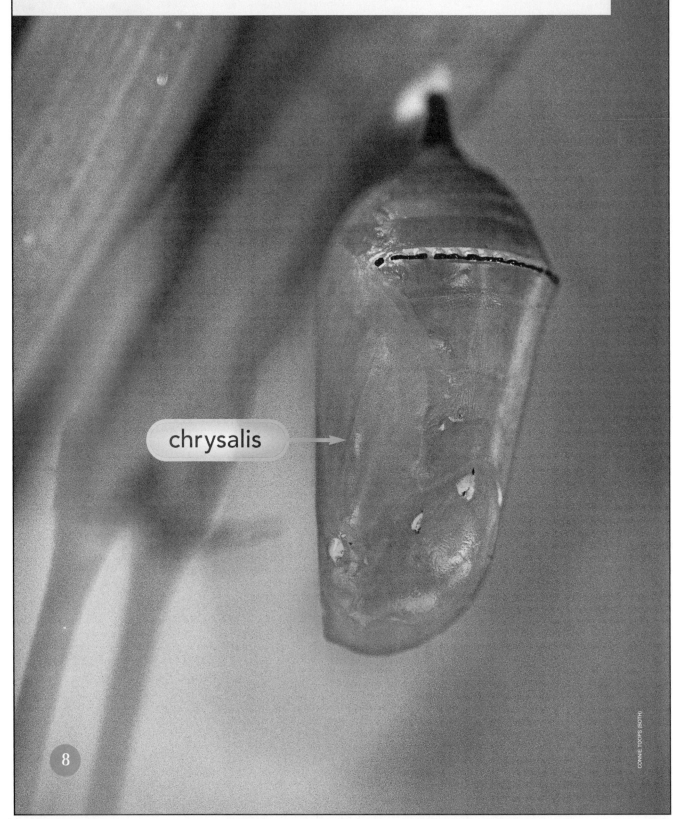

chrysalis

8

The pupa grows wings.
It is a butterfly now.
It comes out of the chrysalis.

pupa

9

The butterfly is tired.
Its wings are wet.
It rests and dries.

CONNIE TOOPS

chrysalis

butterfly

wet wings

10

The butterfly flies away.

CORBIS IMAGES

11

A Butterfly Grows

How does a butterfly grow?

Look at the drawing.

Follow each step.

7 The butterfly flies away.

6 The pupa turns into a butterfly.

5 The caterpillar turns into a pupa.

PRECISION GRAPHICS

12

Up

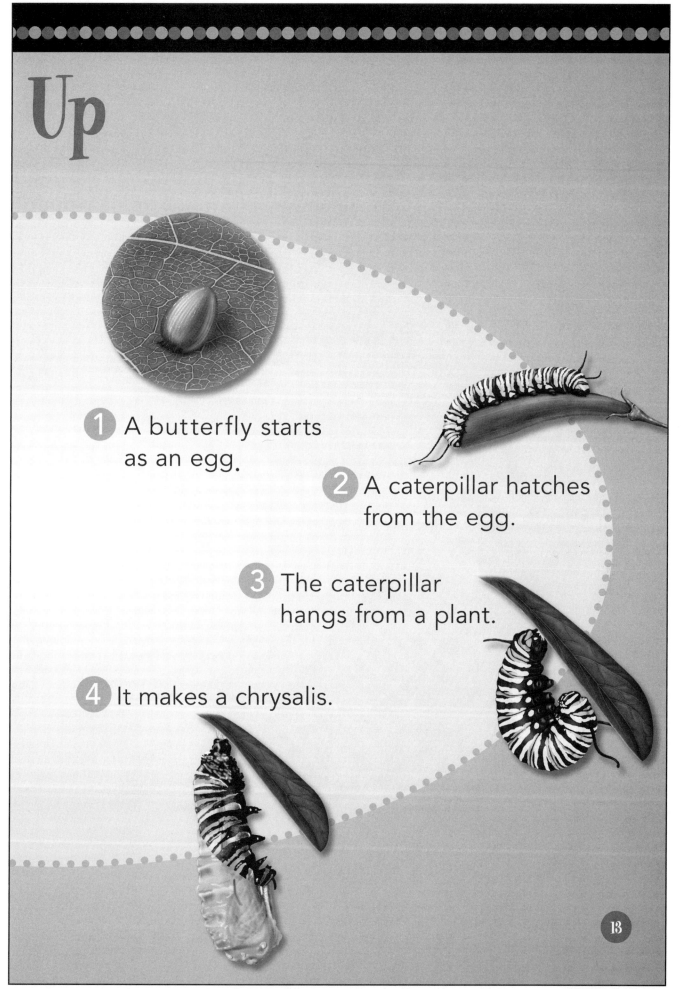

1 A butterfly starts as an egg.

2 A caterpillar hatches from the egg.

3 The caterpillar hangs from a plant.

4 It makes a chrysalis.

Big Picture

Compare the Parts

How are a caterpillar and a butterfly alike?

How are they different?

Caterpillar

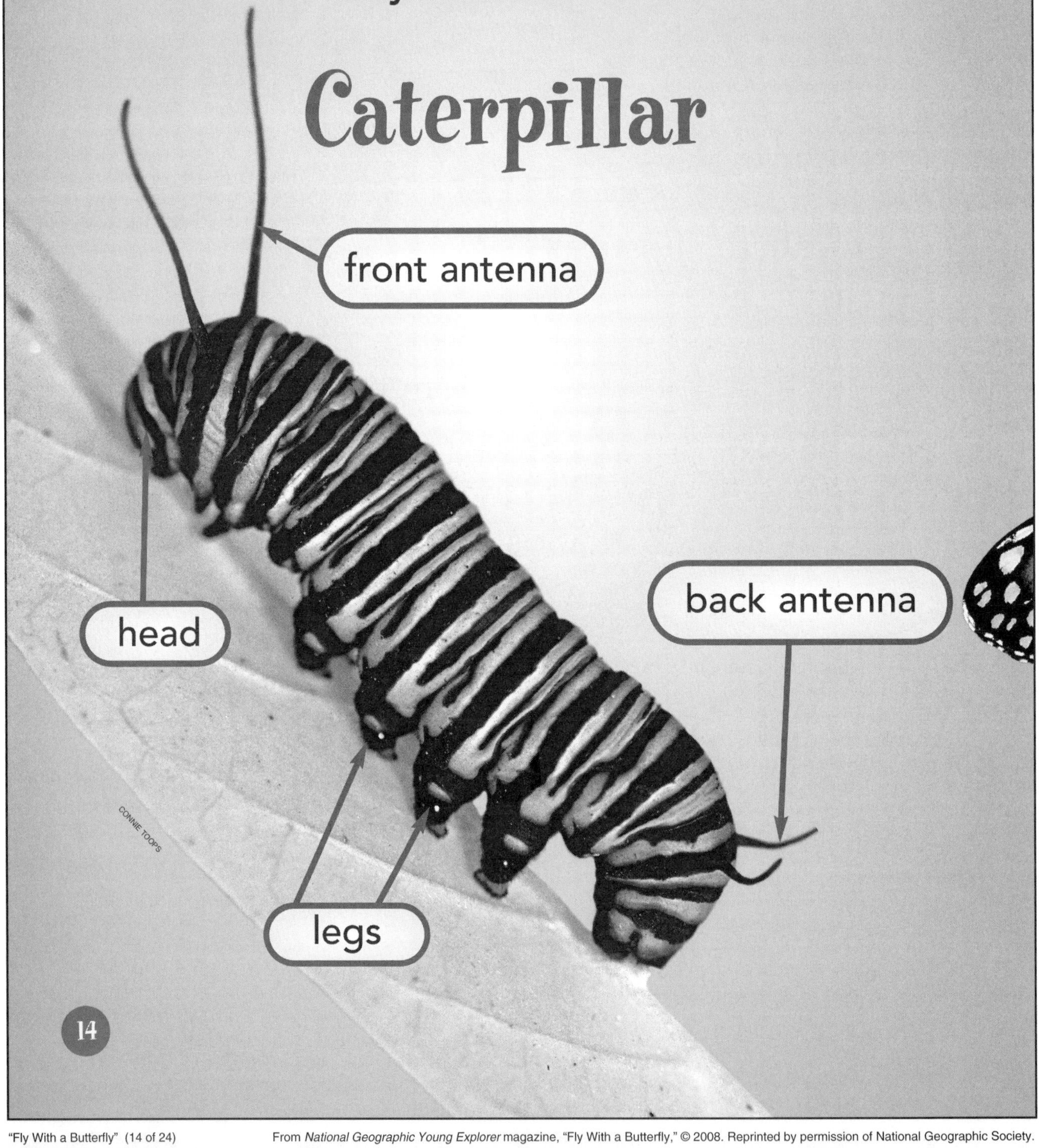
front antenna
head
back antenna
legs
CONNIE TOOPS

Butterfly

head

antenna

legs

wings

15

How Seeds

© BIOS-KLEIN & HUBERT/PETER ARNOLD

16

Spread

Seeds **spread** in many ways.
How does this girl spread seeds?

seed

How does a **plant** spread **seeds**?

How does water spread seeds?

seed

How does a dog spread seeds?

seed

seed

How does a chipmunk spread seeds?
What else spreads seeds?

Words t

butterfly

chrysalis

caterpillar

egg

22

o Explore

plant

seed

pupa

spread

23

NATIONAL GEOGRAPHIC Young Explorer!

Butterfly

She finds a spot. Her stay is brief.
She lays her egg beneath a leaf.

Inside the egg, day after day,
A caterpillar has a way

Of knowing how to stretch and grow.
Once on her own, she likes to show

The kind of trick that nature brings
When she spreads her WINGS!

—J. Patrick Lewis

NATIONAL GEOGRAPHIC YOUNG EXPLORER is a publication of the
NATIONAL GEOGRAPHIC SOCIETY
brought to you in cooperation with the

INTERNATIONAL PAPER FOUNDATION

NATIONAL GEOGRAPHIC SOCIETY
EDUCATION FOUNDATION

Vice President and Publisher:
Francis Downey
Art Director: Karen Thompson
Designer: Kathleen Greuel
Senior Editor: Peter Winkler
Editor: Dana Jensen
Photo Editors:
Mary Ann Price, Miriam Stein
Writer: Barbara Wood
Production Specialist:
Theodore B. Tucker IV
Senior Marketing Manager:
Nikki Lowry

SCHOOL PUBLISHING GROUP
Chief Executive Officer: Sheron Long
President: Samuel Gesumaria
**Director of Design and
Illustrations:** Margaret Sidlosky
Research Manager: Amber Petry
Manager, Publishing Services:
Matt Wascavage
Project Manager: Sean Philpotts

**MANUFACTURING AND
QUALITY CONTROL**
Chief Financial Officer:
Christopher A. Liedel
Vice President: Phillip L. Schlosser
Director: Clifton M. Brown
Postal Director: Kerry Knight

**PUBLISHED BY THE
NATIONAL GEOGRAPHIC SOCIETY**
John M. Fahey, Jr., *President*
Gilbert M. Grosvenor,
Chairman of the Board

**NATIONAL GEOGRAPHIC
YOUNG EXPLORER**
(ISSN 1930-8116) is published seven
times during the school year—September,
October, November–December,
January–February, March, April, May—
by the National Geographic Society,
1145 17th Street NW, Washington, D.C.
20036–4688. Postmaster: Please send
address changes to NATIONAL GEOGRAPHIC
EXPLORER, PO Box 4002865, Des Moines,
IA 50340–2865. Periodical postage paid
at Washington, D.C., and additional
mailing offices.

U.S. Classroom Price: $3.95 per student
per year (10 to 199 subscriptions to the
same address). *U.S. School Price:* $2.50
per student per year (200 or more
subscriptions to the same address).
To subscribe, call 1-800-368-2728.

Cover: A monarch butterfly rests
on a flower. (Photo by Tom and
Pat Leeson.)

**Learn more
about
YOUNG EXPLORER
at**
**nationalgeographic.com
/ngyoungexplorer**

Keep Reading!

a sourcebook of short text

Short Text Titles
and Reading Level Designations

KEY

* Most Accessible Text
** More Challenging Text
*** Most Challenging Text

Watch Me Grow!

Some baby animals hatch from **eggs.** Can you guess what will hatch from this egg?

1.Egg

A **hen** lays an egg. She will sit on the egg to keep it warm.

2.Hatching

A **chick** hatches from the egg.
The chick comes out wet and sticky.
Soon the chick's feathers dry and turn soft and fluffy.

3.Baby chick

A chick loves to eat seeds.
It will grow up quickly.

4.Chicken

The chick's fluffy,
yellow feathers fall out.
It grows new, darker
feathers.
It has a red comb on
its head,
just like its mother!

Glossary

Chick - baby chicken

Egg - a shell that holds the baby chick

Hen - mother chicken

Rooster - father chicken

Did you know?

These hatch from eggs too!

snake

lizard

turtle

alligator

duck

The Bald Eagle

Sharp eyes

Strong, hooked beak

The bald eagle is the national bird.

Light, strong wings

Sharp talons

Tail feathers

9 feet

Eagles do not flap their wings much. They soar and glide with flat wings.

Did You Know **?** The bald eagle builds the biggest nest. The nest is about 9 feet across—taller than two kids!

The Grizzly Bear

Big hump

Small, round ears

Thick, furry coat

Big, wet nose

Long claws

Small tail

Grizzly bears live in forests, meadows, and mountains. They only live in North America.

North America

Grizzly bears
eat grass,
leaves, berries,
and seeds.
They also eat
insects, fish, and
small animals.

All bears can swim.
They are happy in
the water.
They catch fish or
cool off on a hot day.

A baby bear is called a cub.
Mama bears take care of their cubs
for two years.
Mama bears keep their cubs safe,
teach them to fish and hunt,
and play with them!
After two years, they go off to hunt,
fish, and grow up on their own.

The Three Goats

Goats can climb.

Goats can play.

Goats drink water.

Goats eat hay.

Goats are funny.

Goats get sleepy.

Good night, goats.
Good night!

Our Class Pets!

I asked some kids in my class, "Do you have a pet?"
9 kids said yes. 5 kids said no.

Do you have a pet?

Yes	X X X X X X X X X
No	X X X X X

I asked some kids which kind of pet they would like to have.

Favorite Pets

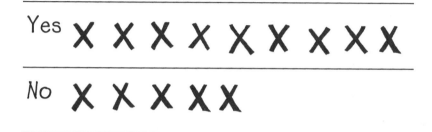

We made a Venn diagram to show where they live.

Where Pets Live

Land   Both   Water

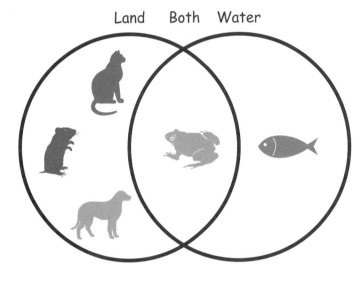

Which is your favorite pet?

Frog

Gerbil

Dog

Fish

Cat

Ask the kids in your class about their pets.

Fill in this graph.

Favorite Pets

Dogs	
Cats	
Frog	
Fish	
Other	

Fill in this Venn diagram.

Where Pets Live

Land   Both   Water

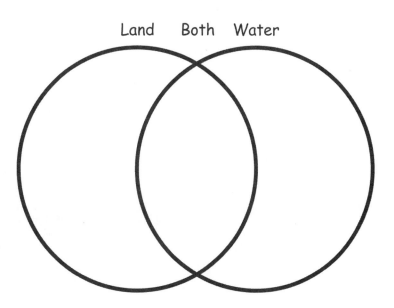

Footprints in the Forest

When you walk in the forest, you might see animal footprints or tracks.

Bobcat

Different animals leave different tracks. Do you want to know what animal walked in the woods before you? Look at the shape of its tracks. Read on to learn about how animals' feet are shaped and how they walk and move.

Fox

Beaver

Deer

Rabbit

Raccoon

A fox leaves footprints like a
small dog.
A fox uses its back legs to
jump high.

A bobcat leaves footprints like a big
house cat.
A bobcat is good at leaping, just
like a cat.

A raccoon has five fingers on
each foot, just like you!
A raccoon's feet help it climb
and swim.

A rabbit's big back feet leave
big footprints.
Its big back feet help it hop.

A beaver has webbed feet.
Its webbed feet help it swim.

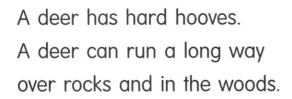

A deer has hard hooves.
A deer can run a long way
over rocks and in the woods.

Whose tracks are these?

(For answers, turn the page upside down.)

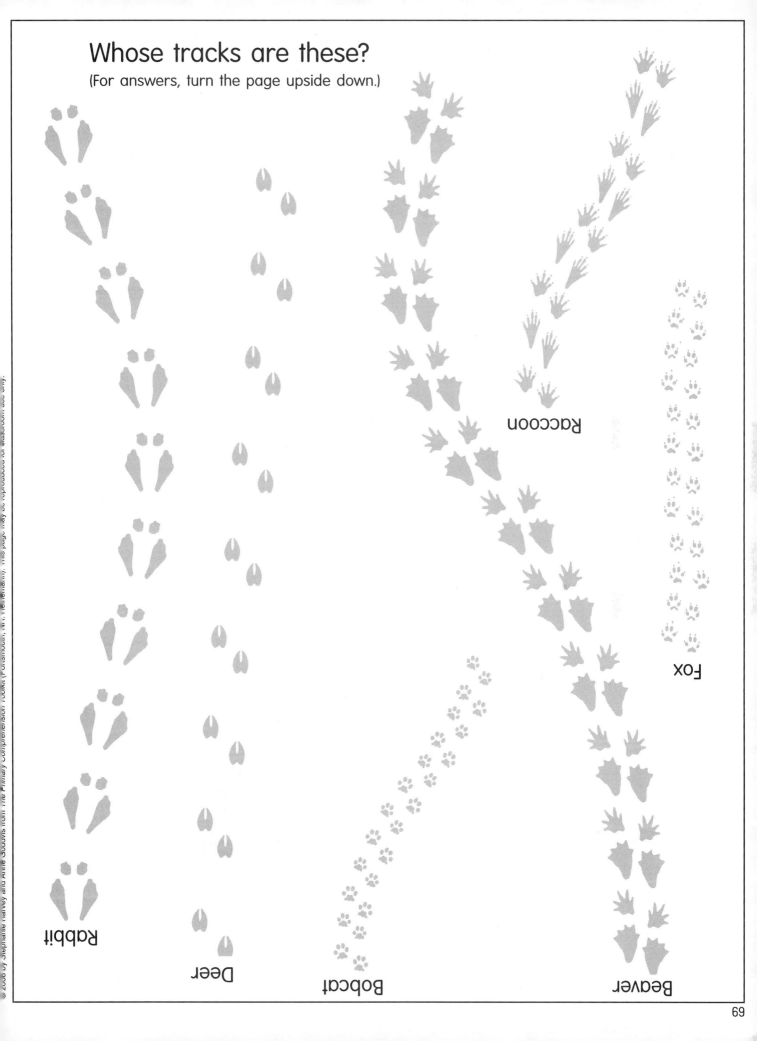

Raccoon

Fox

Rabbit

Deer

Bobcat

Beaver

Symmetry in Nature

Symmetry is all around you in nature.

If you draw a line down the middle

of a leaf, you will find that one half

has the same shape as the other half.

We say the two halves of the leaf

are **symmetrical.**

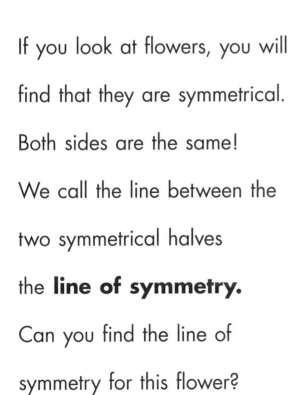

If you look at flowers, you will

find that they are symmetrical.

Both sides are the same!

We call the line between the

two symmetrical halves

the **line of symmetry.**

Can you find the line of

symmetry for this flower?

If you look at insects,
you will see that their bodies
are symmetrical, too.
The beetle and the butterfly
look exactly the same on
both sides of their bodies.

71

Animals have symmetrical bodies, too!

Look at the turtle and panda below.

Can you find the line of symmetry?

Half of the butterfly below is missing.

Draw the other half of the butterfly.

Can you make it symmetrical?

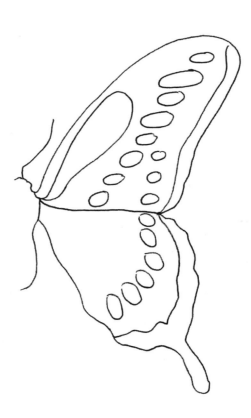

Don't Trash the Earth! Reduce, Reuse, and Recycle

Take care of our world! You can help keep plants, animals, people, and our world clean and healthy with the 3Rs—**Reduce, Reuse, and Recycle**.

Reduce

Reduce means to use less. How?

- Buy things with less paper and plastic packaging. There will be less to throw away!
- Use less electricity by turning off the lights when you leave a room.
- Write on both sides of your paper. You will use one less sheet of paper.

Can you think of other ways to use less?

Reuse

Reuse means to use something again.

- Save grocery bags and use them again.
- Wash out empty glass jars and use them again.

How could *you* use grocery bags or jars again?

Recycle

Recycle means to make something new out of something that has been used. Some things we use every day are made from metal or paper or plastic or glass. Instead of throwing them away after we use them, we can recycle them. We give cans and bottles to people who shred them to make new cans and bottles. We give old paper to people who can use it to make new paper.

- Put empty cans and bottles in the recycle bin.
- Sort paper and put it in the recycle bin.

Recycling gives us new things and makes the world cleaner by reducing trash.

2008 by Stephanie Harvey and Anne Goudvis from *The Primary Comprehension Toolkit* (Portsmouth, NH: Heinemann). This page may be reproduced for classroom use only.

wow!

Did you know that a plastic soda bottle can be made into t-shirts? First the old plastic bottle is cleaned. Then it is chopped up, melted down, and made into fabric for new t-shirts!

Sensing the Seasons

I walk my dog in the spring.
I smell flowers blooming.

I walk my dog in the summer.
I hear birds singing.

I walk my dog in the fall.
I see leaves changing colors.

I walk my dog in the winter.
I feel snow falling.

Where in the United States Do Tornadoes Mostly Happen?

A tornado starts as a powerful storm.

The wind forms a spinning cloud shaped like a funnel.

The funnel cloud moves and destroys everything in its path.

Many tornadoes happen in the United States.

Most of them happen in the Great Plains area, in the middle of the country.

This area is called **Tornado Alley**.

What states are in Tornado Alley?

Where is Tornado Alley?

Key

places where
tornadoes
often happen

Tornado
Alley

States shown on map: ME, NH, MA, RI, CT, VT, NY, NJ, DE, MD, PA, WV, VA, NC, OH, SC, MI, KY, TN, AL, GA, FL, IN, IL, WI, MO, AR, MS, LA, MN, IA, KS, OK, TX, ND, SD, NE, CO, WY, NM, MT, UT, ID, AZ, WA, OR, NV, CA, AK, HI

What's the Weather Out There?

Anyone can tell the weather by looking out a window. A **meteorologist** is a scientist who studies the **weather.** Casey Anderson is a meteorologist. He answered a few questions about the weather.

What tools do you use?

I use a **thermometer** to measure how hot or how cold it is outside. I look at special pictures from a **radar** to see the rain or snow. A radar is an electronic tool that measures how far a storm is from a town and which direction it is moving. These radar pictures help me predict the weather.

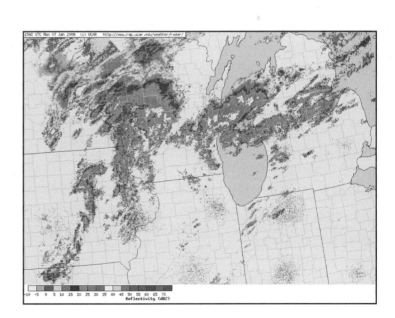

What are clouds?

Clouds are the white or gray fluffs you see in the sky. They are made up of tiny drops of water and ice. The droplets are so small and light that they can float in the air. Sometimes, if the wind is fast enough, you can even watch the clouds move. Clouds can come in all sizes and shapes. They can be near the ground or way up high. Different types of clouds cause different kinds of weather. We would not have rain, rainbows, or snow without clouds.

When do rainbows happen?

You can see a **rainbow** in the sky when bright sunlight bounces off raindrops. Sunlight is made of many colors. When the sun's rays enter a raindrop, the raindrop acts like a mirror. The rays bend and reflect the light so you can see the colors as they curve across the sky in a rainbow. You can even make your own rainbow with a garden hose or water sprinkler on a sunny day.

What are snowflakes?

Snowflakes are made of tiny pieces of ice called ice crystals. Each crystal has six sides. The crystals grow in clouds when the temperature is below freezing. The ice crystals form around tiny bits of dust that have been carried high in the sky by the wind. As the snow crystals grow, they become heavier and fall toward the ground as snowflakes. Sometimes you can see perfect ice crystals in the snow. But most of the time, the snow falls as large clumps of crystals. There are as many as 200 ice crystals in a single snowflake!

Words to know:

cloud–a large group of very tiny drops of water or ice crystals

meteorologist–a scientist who studies the weather

radar–an electronic tool that measures the direction and distance of storms

rainbow–a band of many colors in the sky

snowflake–a group of tiny ice crystals

temperature–how hot or cold it is outside

thermometer–a tool that measures the temperature

weather–how warm or cold, wet or dry, or clear or stormy it is outside

Families:
The Things We Do Together

bake

cook

eat

walk

play

work

read

talk

hug

My Neighborhood

This is where
We get our books.
This is where
My mommy cooks.

This is where
We get our mail.
This is where
Our food's on sale.

This is where
I read and write.
This is where
I sleep at night.

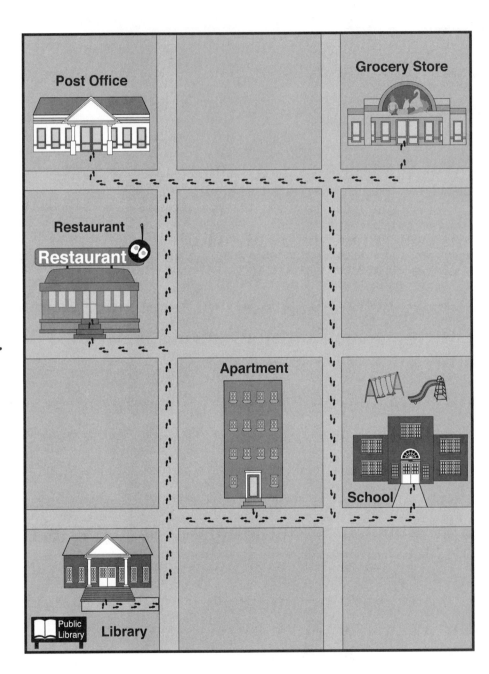

We Take Care of Our Pet

I give him water.

ARE YOU THIRSTY?

I give him food.

ARE YOU HUNGRY?

YUM!!

I give him hugs!

Who lives in the zoo?

Who lives at the aquarium?

Who lives at the petting farm?

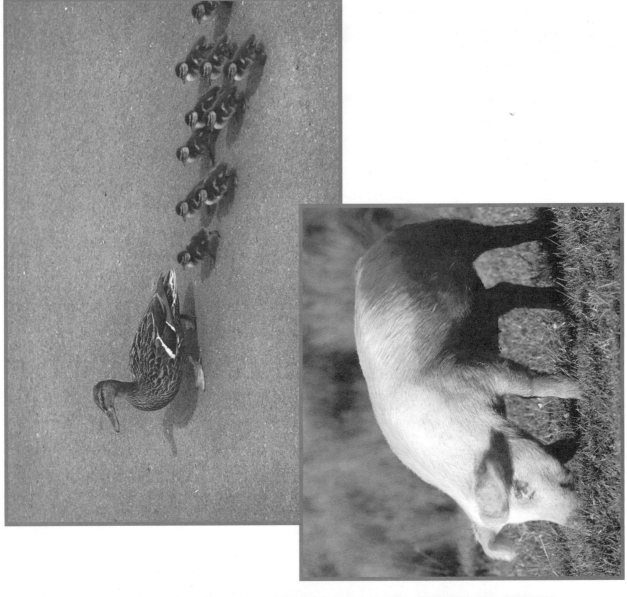

Who lives in a house?

apartment

farmhouse

Where Do We Live?

houseboat

mobile home

grass hut

yurt

© 2008 by Stephanie Harvey and Anne Goudvis from *The Primary Comprehension Toolkit* (Portsmouth, NH: Heinemann). This page may be reproduced for classroom use only.

Community Helpers

"My dad is a **policeman**. He helps keep us safe."

"My mom is a **doctor**. She helps sick people."

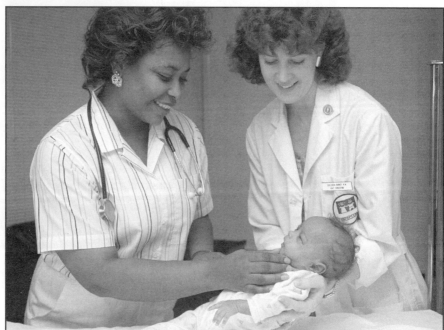

"My dad is a **teacher**.
He helps kids learn."

"My mom is a **firefighter**.
She puts out fires."

"My dad is a **bus driver**.
He drives kids to school."

"My mom is a **librarian**.
She helps us find books to read."

A New Home

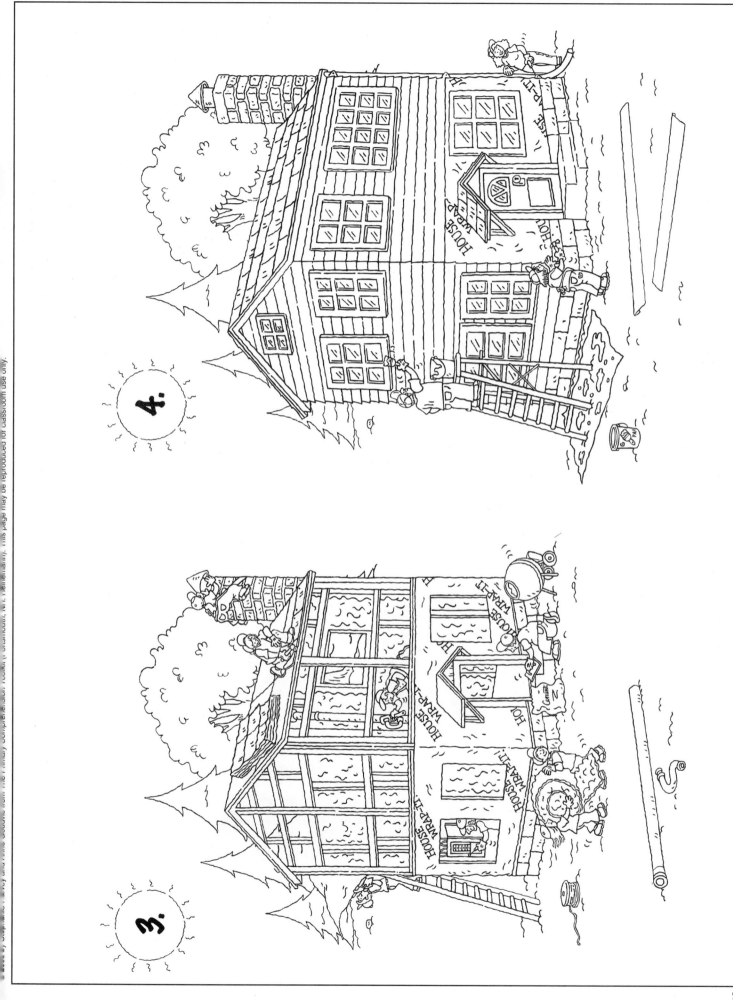

Carpenter

Carpenters work with wood.

They use tools to build things.

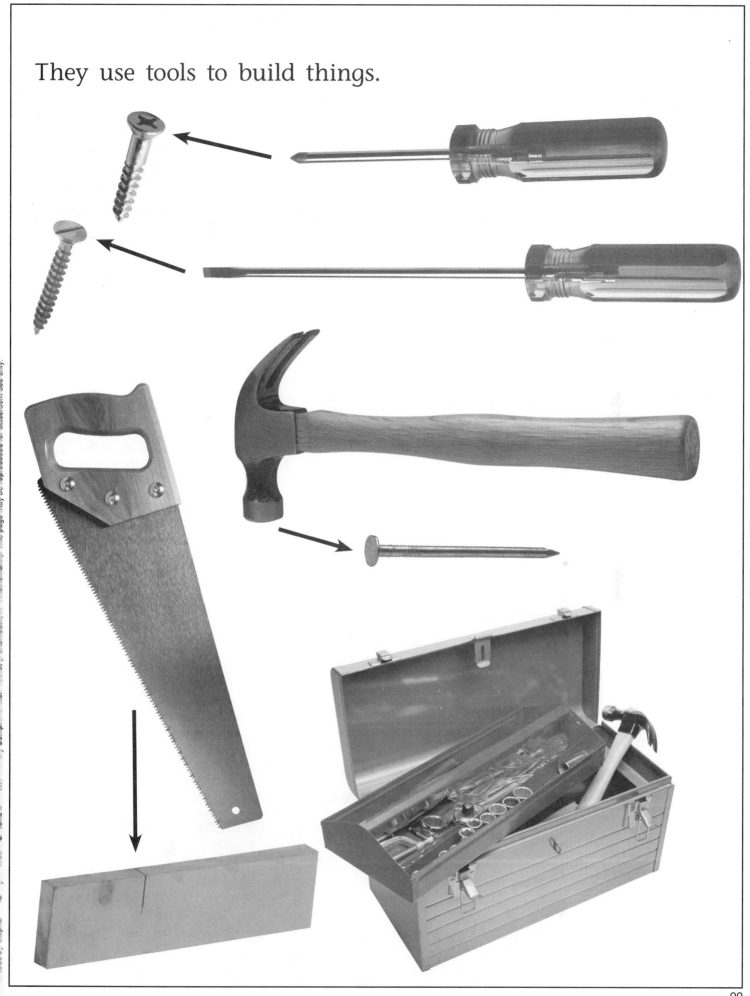

Off to School

Good morning!
I'm in first grade.
I get myself ready
to learn every morning.

1 I eat breakfast.

2 I brush my teeth.

3 I put on my coat and my backpack.

4 I'm ready to go to school!

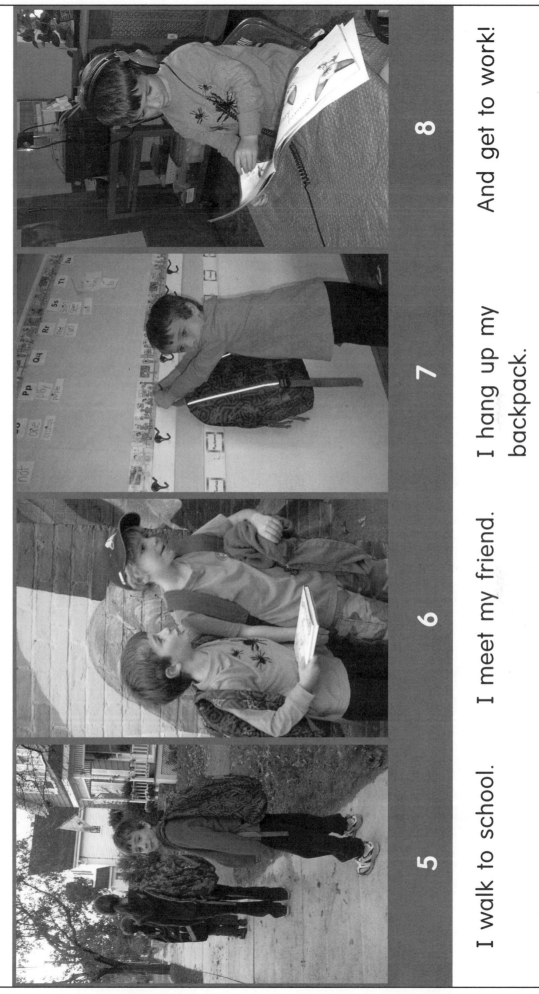

5 I walk to school.

6 I meet my friend.

7 I hang up my backpack.

8 And get to work!

Ask the Farmer!

What does a farmer do?

Farmers work hard.
A farmer milks the cows.
He feeds the animals.
He grows corn and vegetables.

What does a farmer use?

A farmer uses a tractor.
He drives a truck.
He pulls a wagon.

What do farm animals eat?

Farm animals eat food
grown on the farm.
Cows eat hay and corn.
Chickens eat seeds and grain.

Where do farm animals sleep?

The cows sleep in the barn.
The chickens sleep
in the chicken coop.

Tractor

The Country

orchard

silo

barn

chickens

pigs

cows

pond   ducks

tractor

farmhouse

cat

tree

Pick your own
strawberries

The City

stores

BANK

Flowers

TOYS

FarmFresh Milk

truck

tree

pond

park

streetlight

ducks

car

bus

apartments

Dictionary

apartments

barn

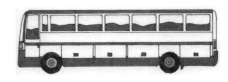

bus

car

cat

chickens

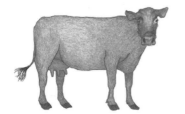

cow

orchard

pig

stores

streetlight

tractor

Postcards from the Desert Museum

Arizona- Sonora Desert Museum

Monday

Hi, Nick,

Grandpa and I went to the Desert Museum today. It's not like most museums. It's outside and has lots of desert plants and animals. This cactus, called a Saguaro, is very tall. If I stand on Grandpa's shoulders, I still can't reach the top!

Love, Gram

POSTCARD

Nick Vetrano

15 Baker Rd.

Hometown, KY

42792

Tuesday

Hi, Dan,
Yesterday at the Desert Museum we went to the raptor show. Raptors are birds that hunt for meat to eat. We saw trained hawks and owls flying free. This owl is perched on its trainer's hand.

                    Love, Gram

Dan
15 B
Hom
4279

Wednesday

Hi, Jen,
We went back to the Desert Museum today. We stayed indoors with the arachnids: spiders and scorpions. Ugh! I was glad they were in tanks! One scorpion looked a lot like this.

                    Love, Gram

Jen
15
Hc
4

Arizona- Sonora Desert Museum

Thursday

Hi, Kim,
The Desert Museum is like
a zoo. It has homes for
mountain goats, bears,
beavers, and lots more.
These prairie dogs live in
an underground burrow.
They made me laugh when
they barked because they
looked just like kids
talking with each other.
                    Love, Gram

POSTCARD

Kim Vetrano

15 Baker Rd.

Hometown, KY

42792

Prairie Dog Homes

Prairie dogs live in a home
under the ground.
Their home is called a **burrow.**

Team Work

Prairie dogs work together
to dig their burrow.
They use their sharp claws to dig.
First they dig a hole.
Then they push the dirt out of it.
The dirt piles up into a big mound.

Tiny Tunnels

The prairie dog burrow
has tunnels and rooms.
Prairie dogs dig tunnels
just wide enough for them
to fit through. They also
dig a second entrance for
quick escapes from predators.

Rooms for Different Uses

The rooms are wider.
They have different uses.
There is a room for sleeping
and a room for storing food.
There is even a bathroom!
Near the top, there is
a listening room.

Why do you think prairie dogs
have a listening room?

Inside a Prairie Dog Burrow

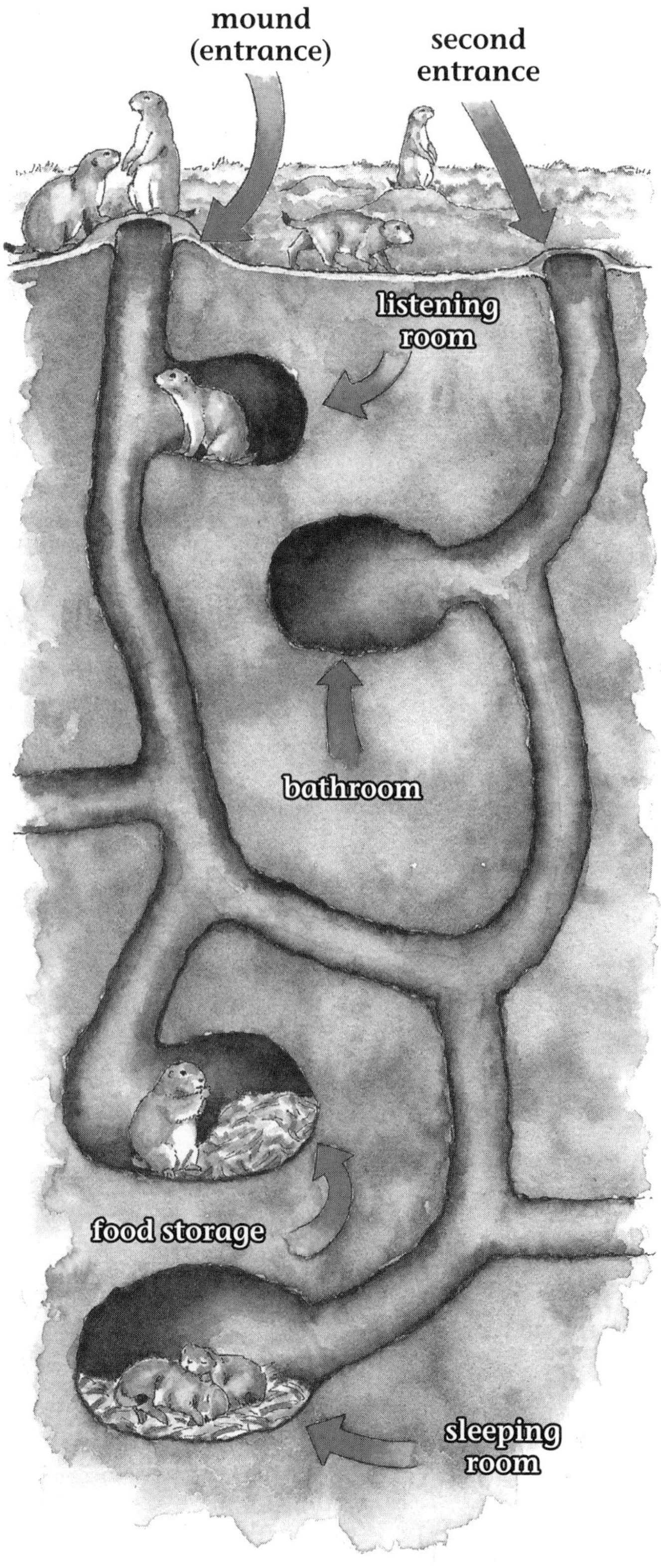

mound
(entrance)

second
entrance

listening
room

bathroom

food storage

sleeping
room

Answer:
Prairie dogs have a listening room so they
can stay safe below the ground while they
listen for predators.

5 Hill Street

Hometown, WI 53700

August 21, 2008

Dear Aunt Pat,

Thanks for taking me to visit
Washington, D.C. last weekend!
I had fun on our trip to the city.
My favorite things were
the Washington Monument
and the White House. I
couldn't believe how tall the
Washington Monument is! It was
very exciting to see the house
where the President of the
United States lives and works.

Some day I want to live in a city.
But now I'm going out to the barn
to feed the chickens.

Love,

Sarah

P.S. Here are some pictures I took.

Washington Monument

White House

Counting Fruit Salad

 **1** bowl

 **2** pieces of plum

 **3** strawberries

 **4** slices of apple

5 slices of pear

6 pieces of orange

7 grapes

8 pieces of banana

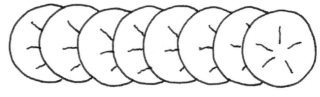

stir **9** times

10 EAT!

Make a Sandwich!

I like bread.

I like peanut butter.

I like jelly.

119

What Time Is It?

Celebrations Timeline

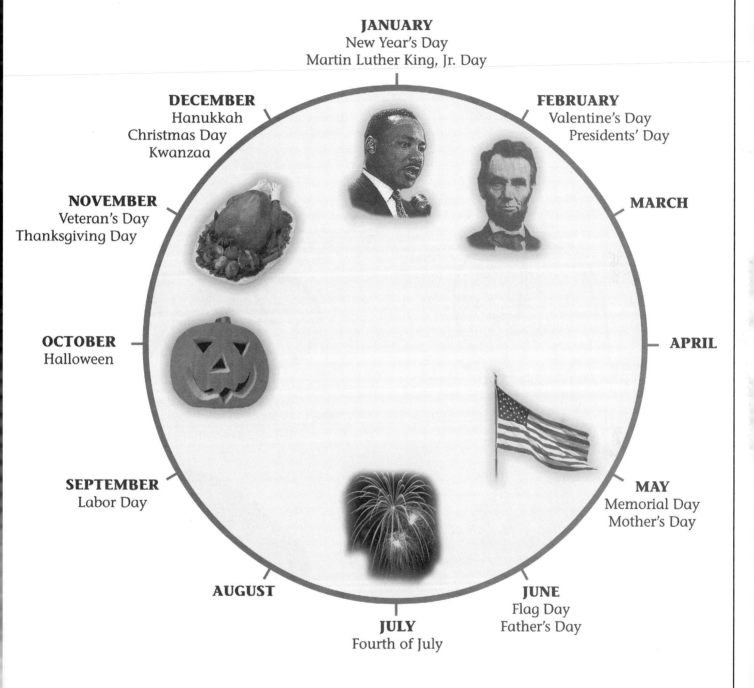

JANUARY
New Year's Day
Martin Luther King, Jr. Day

DECEMBER
Hanukkah
Christmas Day
Kwanzaa

FEBRUARY
Valentine's Day
Presidents' Day

NOVEMBER
Veteran's Day
Thanksgiving Day

MARCH

OCTOBER
Halloween

APRIL

SEPTEMBER
Labor Day

MAY
Memorial Day
Mother's Day

AUGUST

JUNE
Flag Day
Father's Day

JULY
Fourth of July

Mark your birthday
on the timeline.

Mark a special holiday
your family celebrates.

OLD and NEW

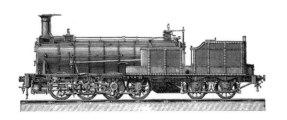

Meet Eric Carle

Photographer: Paul Shoul

Eric Carle writes stories
and makes the pictures, too.

He is an author and illustrator.

The Very Hungry Caterpillar
is one of Eric Carle's books.
He also wrote **The Very Busy
Spider**, **The Grouchy Ladybug**,
and many more books for kids.

THE VERY
HUNGRY
CATERPILLAR
by Eric Carle

His pictures are called **collages.**
First he paints the paper.
Next he cuts out shapes.
Then he pastes them together.

You can make collages, too!

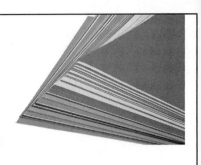

I Like Art!

Crayons,
Markers,
Glue stick,
Paint

Scissors,
Paper,
Pencils, too

Are all the things
I use to make

A special picture
Just for you!

A Stick Puppet Play

duck

rabbit

cat

monster

Make A Stick Puppet

You need

paper   a pencil   scissors   tape   a straw

1. Trace.

2. Cut.

3. Tape.

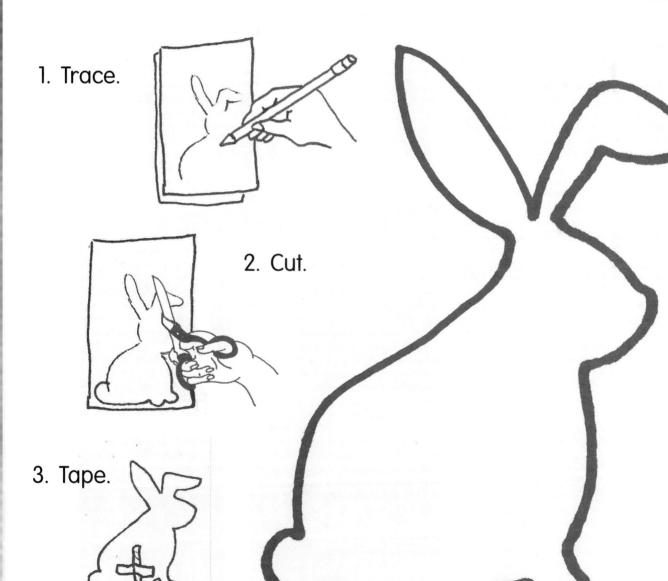

Totem Poles, Family Stories

Everyone likes to hear family stories. Maybe your parents or grandparents tell old family stories. The American Indians who lived on the northwest coast of the United States many years ago did not have a written language. They carved pictures into tall pieces of wood. These carvings are called **totem poles.** The pictures on a totem pole remind American Indians of their family story. It is how a family passes on stories and legends.

Totem poles have animals carved on them from top to bottom. These special animals are part of the family's story. Every totem pole is different because each tells a different family's story. A totem pole for one family might have beavers, butterflies, wolves, and frogs carved upon it. The totem pole for a different family is carved with whales, bears, ravens, and owls. The carvings may not look like these animals to us, but they do to the American Indians who carve them.

Can you see the different animals in the totem pole?

Did you know?

A totem pole can be 70 feet tall! That is taller than many schools!

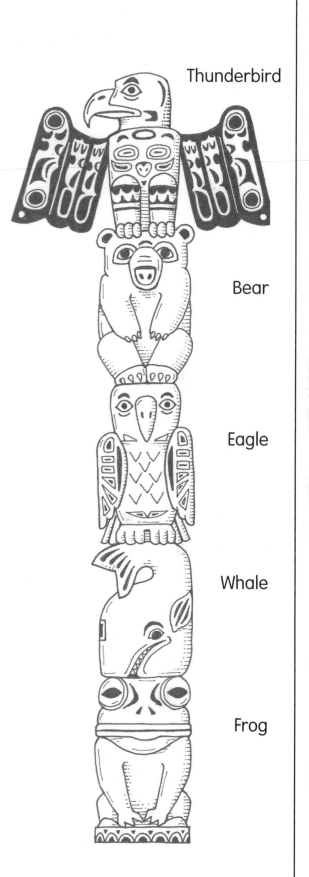

Thunderbird

Bear

Eagle

Whale

Frog

Kids at Play

On the Mat

On the Field

On the Track

On the Playground

In the Water

Up a Wall

In the Woods

On the Ice

In the Snow

Having a Ball Playing Soccer

I like to play soccer. I play on a team called the Panthers.

Playing soccer is fun! Being a Panther takes teamwork.

My coach teaches us how to play together.

We run on the field.

We pass the ball to our teammates.

We kick the ball hard. Sometimes our team even scores a goal!

The best part of playing soccer is being with *my* friends.

Maybe some day I will play for the *U.S. Women's Team* in the World Cup.

But for now, I like being a Panther.

Let's Go Hiking!

You can hike in the woods.

You can hike in the mountains.

You can hike with a pack on your back.

You can hike with a stick.

You can sit and rest.

You can eat a snack, too.

We love to hike!

Bibliography

Trade and Picture Books

Picture books abound, so many in fact, that creating a list can be daunting and even a little presumptuous. Certainly you will be delighted at some of our inclusions. Yet you may be dismayed at the absence of some of your favorites. We offer a smattering of books we love for you to share with your kids. These are by no means the only books we care about, but reality prevailed here; we simply had to stop somewhere! Our list is peppered with some old classics as well as some hot-off-the-press titles. But in the end, remember to share any book you care about. Passion is contagious! Kids will jump right in when you invite them into a book you dearly love!

Consider the following as you match great books to the needs and interests of kids:

- Kids need books they can sink their teeth into, so we have selected books on a variety of topics that present important ideas and issues in child-friendly ways. We also recommend a list of nonfiction authors who specialize in either social studies or science topics.

- Books on these common curricular topics in science and social studies can expand and enhance reading, writing, and thinking across the curriculum.

- Many of these books are most appropriate for read-alouds and discussions. Suggestions of books in several series also lend themselves to self-selected reading on a wide range of levels.

- Fiction, historical fiction, and even poetry are important sources of information—kids learn a lot from thoughtful, well-written text in a variety of genres.

- Informational text with original formats, striking features, and stunning pictures and photographs make enticing read-alouds. They become mentor texts for children as they begin to write nonfiction themselves.

- The concepts in these books can be challenging. Every text should be thoroughly previewed with your kids in mind to determine if they are appropriate, especially for the youngest learners.

Social Studies

Culture, History, and Contemporary Issues

Great picture books for reading aloud and shared reading

Aliki. *Marianthe's Story: Painted Words/Spoken Memories.* New York: Greenwillow Books, 1998.
A little girl from Greece shares her story with her classmates, first in paintings. As she learns English, she begins to tell her story in words. The book is two books in one, begin by reading **Painted Words,** then flip it over to continue Marianthe's story of her experiences in a new culture, reading **Spoken Memories.**

Borden, Louise. *Off to First Grade.* New York: Simon and Schuster, 2008.
Every school-aged child can relate to this charming story of heading off to first grade, with all of the anxiety and anticipation that go along with that. Great book for teaching kids to make connections.

Borden, Louise. *The Journey that Saved Curious George: The True Wartime Escape of Margret and H.A. Rey.* Boston: Houghton Mifflin, 2005.
Learn all about the Rey's amazing escape from Nazi-occupied France in this large format book that resembles a travel journal and includes full-color illustrations, origi-

nal photos, actual ticket stubs, and more. A wonderful book for Curious George fans of all ages. Terrific text for teaching nonfiction features and primary sources.

Borden, Louise. *The A+ Custodian.* New York: Simon and Schuster, 2004.
A book that celebrates one of the most important people in the school, the custodian. Great to help kids become aware of the necessity of keeping the school clean and organized and recognizing the importance of this community helper.

Borden, Louise and Mary Kay Kroeger. *Fly High: The Story of Bessie Coleman.* New York: McElderry, 2001.
The inspiring story of Bessie Coleman, the first woman pilot and the first African American pilot. Written in a poetic, lyrical style, this gripping narrative gives us a peek into the life of the brave woman from Chicago who broke two major barriers.

Bruchac, Joseph. *Squanto's Journey.* San Diego: Harcourt, 2007.
A fascinating story about the famous Native American so closely associated with the First Thanksgiving. This narrative reveals many surprising twists and turns in his life which make his contribution even more remarkable.

Bunting, Eve. *Fly Away Home.* New York: Clarion, 1991.
Tough times have forced a boy and his father to take up residence in the airport to stay off the street while the father tries to find work. Questions abound. Why are they in the airport? Will they ever get a home? How do people become homeless? Readers cannot stop wondering about these thoughts and more.

Bunting, Eve. *My Red Balloon.* Honesdale: Boyds Mills Press, 2005.
It is the day a young boy's father arrives home from overseas. Feelings of excitement and apprehension will be familiar to children who have parents returning from current conflicts.

Bunting, Eve. *One Green Apple.* New York: Clarion, 2006.
This is the story of a young Muslim immigrant, written from her perspective. Farah is the new girl at school and does not speak or understand the language of her classmates. The class travels to an apple orchard where she discovers familiar "sounds."

Bunting, Eve. *Jin Woo.* New York: Clarion, 2001.
A young boy's parents are adopting a baby from Korea and the boy, also adopted, is less than overjoyed. With sensitivity and humor, Bunting writes of the boy's emotional journey from dread, to acceptance, and then affection.

Coles, Robert. *The Story of Ruby Bridges.* New York: Scholastic, 1995.
As the only African American child to attend an all-white school, six-year-old Ruby bravely walked through crowds of protesters each day in New Orleans in 1956. Over the course of the year, Ruby stood her ground, her teacher supported her and the other children returned, integrating the schools despite protests and problems.

Cooney, Barbara. *Eleanor.* New York: Viking, 1996.
"From the beginning the baby was a disappointment to her mother." So begins this account of Eleanor Roosevelt's childhood. Text will inspire much discussion about how this lonely child went on to become such an impressive woman in light of her early years.

Cruise, Robin. *Little Mama Forgets.* New York: Farrar, Straus and Giroux, 2006.
The poignant story of a little girl and her beloved grandmother who suffers age-related memory loss. The author explores the tender relationship between these two characters "crisscrossing in the universe" with the girl growing stronger and the grandmother forgetting more each day. And yet, the reader experiences the joy of their love and affection.

Fleming, Candace. *Boxes for Katje.* New York: Farrar, Straus and Giroux, 2003.
Based on a true story about Holland after World War II. Boxes of supplies and necessities sent from people in a small town in Indiana help a young girl and her family survive a terrible winter. In the spring, the grateful Dutch reciprocate, sending a box full of surprises—tulip bulbs, of course—which grace the generous town for years to come.

Garland, Sherry. *The Lotus Seed.* San Diego: Harcourt Brace, 1993.
The story of a young woman who flees Vietnam, taking a lotus seed as a remembrance of her country. Her dangerous journey and life in a new land with her family illustrate the importance of family strength and tradition. Second graders will appreciate this, probably not for kindergartners.

Hopkins, Lee Bennett. *Got Geography!* New York: Greenwillow Books, 2006.
"If you've got geography, you're ready for adventure . . ." Fun selection of poems to be enjoyed by all ages.

Hopkinson, Deborah. *Saving Strawberry Farm.* New York: Greenwillow Books, 2005.
"The sun was so mean that summer, it seemed to chase all the clouds away." Thus begins a beautifully written and illustrated story of a child who learns about the importance of thriftiness and helping others. He eventually helps to save a neighbor's farm as his town comes together for a penny auction. Provides a clear, understandable view of the Depression and hard times.

Johnston, Tony. *Sunsets of the West.* New York: G.P. Putnam's Sons, 2002.
Watercolor illustrations add to the engaging story of a family on a six-month westward journey in a covered wagon.

Jules, Jacqueline. *No English.* Ann Arbor: Mitten Press, 2007.
Blanca, the new second grader from Argentina, speaks "No English." Her classmates learn a lesson about "differences" and communication. Diana and Blanca begin to understand each other and forge a special friendship.

Krull, Kathleen. *Harvesting Hope: the Story of Cesar Chavez.* San Diego: Harcourt Brace, 2003.
Beautifully written and illustrated, this book on a towering figure in the fight for social justice and workers' rights includes an author's note that provides information on the life and times of Cesar Chavez. Also available in Spanish.

Lindbergh, Reeve. *My Little Grandmother Often Forgets.* Cambridge: Candlewick Press, 2007.
This sweet, simple, rhyming text focuses on the relationship between a grandmother dealing with memory loss and her patient, loving grandson. It is based on the author's own experience and offers readers a positive, accepting, and honest viewpoint. Watercolors add to the tone of piece.

McGrath, Barbara Barbieri. *The Storm: Students of Biloxi, Mississippi Remember Hurricane Katrina.* Watertown: Charlesbridge, 2006.
The author visited Biloxi not long after Hurricane Katrina and arranged for communities to donate books as the schools began the long recovery process. Teachers in Biloxi encouraged their kids to write and draw about their experiences to begin healing from the tragic events. This book, a collection of their stories and illustrations, demonstrates the children's resilience and their eagerness to share what happened with other children.

Madrigal, Antonio Hernandez. *Erandi's Braids.* New York: Putnam, 1999.
A moving story about a seven-year-old Mexian girl's willingness to sell her hair to help her financially-strapped mother. The story is based on the hair-selling practice of the 1940s and 1950s. Questions will abound. Familiar-looking illustrations by Tomie dePaola.

Michelson, Richard. *Across the Alley.* New York: G.P. Putnam's Sons, 2006.
Abe and Willie are next door neighbors and, secretly, best friends. Their friendship is a secret because in old-time Brooklyn black children and Jewish children didn't play together. When their families learn what is going on, Willie and Abe bring their families and communities together. A great read about the power of friendship to bridge cultural and racial divides.

Rappaport, Doreen. *Martin's Big Words: The Life of Martin Luther King, Jr.* New York: Scholastic, 2001.
The story of Martin Luther King's life, who the author describes as determined to use "big words," even as a child. The biography is punctuated with compelling short quotes from King and remarkable illustrations by Bryan Collier.

Raven, Margot Theis. *Mercedes and the Chocolate Pilot.* Chelsea: Sleeping Bear Press, 2002.
A true story about the Berlin Airlift following World War II. As part of the humanitarian mission that flew in supplies for the people of West Berlin, an American pilot drops candies that give the children a bit of joy and hope in a difficult time. And one seven-year-old girl wrote to the Chocolate Pilot, initiating a friendship that continued over the years.

Say, Allen. *Grandfather's Journey.* Boston: Houghton Mifflin, 1993.
In this Caldecott Award winner, Allen Say, like his grandfather, finds that "the moment I am in one country, I am homesick for the other." The story moves between two cultures, describing his grandfather's life in Japan and his adventures in the United States.

Sheth, Kahmira. *My Dadima Wears a Sari.* Atlanta: Peachtree, 2007.
Though now living in America, Rupa's grandmother prefers to wear her traditional saris. Rupa learns all the wonderful things that saris can do and be. Watercolors add to this touching story. Photographs showing how to wrap a sari are included at the end.

Sisulu, Elinor. *The Day Gogo Went to Vote.* Boston: Little, Brown and Company, 1996.
In South Africa in 1994, great-grandmother Gogo, who is one hundred years old, takes her great-granddaughter Thembi with her to vote. Gogo's relatives say she is too old to go, but she insists. This story is about the South African election that elected Nelson Mandela as president.

Sneve, Virginia Driving Hawk. *Dancing Teepees.* New York: Holiday House, 1989.
Short poems selected by the author include songs to the blue elk, the stars in the sky, and other aspects of the natural world. This accessible collection stimulates discussion of Native American values, traditions, and beliefs.

Stock, Catherine. *Where Are You Going, Manyoni?* New York: HarperCollins, 1993.
Join Manyoni on her morning walk to school through the African veld. Beautiful watercolor pictures and descriptions of all Manyoni sees and hears present a charming peek into the life of a young child who lives in Zimbabwe.

Van Leeuwen, Jean. *Going West.* New York: Dial, 1992.
Told from the point of view of seven-year-old Hannah, the simple but descriptive text tells the story of hardships and building a new life on the American plains. Harsh weather and loneliness challenge the family, but springtime brings hope.

Williams, Karen Lynn. *When Africa Was Home.* New York: Orchard Books, 1991.
When a young child returns to the United States, he misses the warm African village where he spent his early years. A wonderful book that evokes the experience of belonging to and feeling at home in a different culture.

Woodson, Jacqueline. *The Other Side.* New York: G.P. Putnam's Sons, 2001.
The powerful story of two neighbor girls, one white and one black, whose friendship grows despite the "fence" of segregation that separates them. A great story for prompting discussions of prejudice, racism, friendship, loyalty, and many other important topics.

Social Studies Series

Good books for guided and independent reading, in addition to reading aloud and shared reading

David Adler's *A Picture Book Biography* series (Holiday House) highlights a wide variety of famous people. The list goes on and on! Books are written as narratives, usually chronologically, and are good for read alouds.

De Angelis, Therese. *First Peoples* series. Mankato: Capstone Press. *The Navajo: Weavers of the Southwest* (2004) and others.
Individual books about the Navajo Weavers of the Southwest, The Pueblo—Southwestern Potters, The Inuit—Ivory Carvers of the Far North and other Native American nations and cultures. The books focus on the past experiences and traditions as well as the current lives of native peoples.

Sneve, Virginia Driving Hawk. *The Hopis.* New York: Holiday House, 1995.
A series that presents traditional and present-day Native American life. Individual books on the Hopi, Navajo, Cherokee, Iroquois, and other nations include cultural information, a bit about myths and stories, and information about ceremonies and the arts that portray these peoples' rich heritage.

First Biographies series and *Our World* series. Mankato: Capstone Press.
Independent readers will enjoy the information, photographs, and readability of these. Many subjects and people are included. Also check out Puffin's *Easy to Read* biography series.

Lives and Times series from Heinemann (Heinemann Library) tell the stories of famous people and use photographs and art from the time. Nonfiction features include table of contents, timelines, index, and a glossary (words are bold-faced within text).

Social Studies Authors

Some writers who have authored nonfiction, biographies, historical fiction, and realistic fiction that are of particular interest to primary grade kids:

David Adler	Kathleen Krull
Louise Borden	Kathryn Lasky
Eve Bunting	Andrea Davis Pinkney
Byrd Baylor	Patricia Polocco
Tomie de Paola	Allen Say
Russell Freedman	Jeanette Winter

Science

Animals, Habitats, Ecology, Weather, Space, etc.

Great nonfiction trade books for reading aloud and shared reading

Aillaud, Cindy Lou. *Recess at 20 Below.* Anchorage: Alaska Northwest Books, 2005.
In Barrow, Alaska, school kids go out to recess when it is 20 Below Zero! Kids in the lower 48 are both stunned and entranced by the photos and text in this charming book and they learn bundles about life in a very cold place. Available in *The Primary Comprehension Toolkit Trade Book Pack.*

Arnosky, Jim. *Babies in the Bayou.* New York: GP Putnam's Sons, 2007.
Limited text, though a thought-provoking read aloud for K–1 readers. "Bayou," itself, is a fun word to know and say (!) and is probably a habitat readers may not know. They will relate to the care, teaching, and protection that different mothers provide their offspring.

Aston, Dianna. **An Egg is Quiet.** San Francisco: Chronicle, 2006.
Poetically written text and elegant illustrations will force readers to think differently about eggs. From quiet eggs to noisy eggs, from colorful eggs to clever eggs, this is a celebration of their variety. Egg facts are interspersed throughout the text.

Atkins, Jeannine. **Aani and the Tree Huggers.** New York: Lee and Low Books, 1995.
This story is based on real events in northern India in the 1970's, when women literally hugged and thus saved the trees. As a result of that, today more regulations are in place to protect endangered lands and to plant more trees.

Bang, Molly. **My Light.** New York: Scholastic/Blue Sky, 2004.
Molly Bang's distinctive style will appeal to readers. The creation of electricity is traced, beginning with the energy from the sun.

Bauer, Marion Dane. **A Mama for Owen.** New York: Simon and Schuster, 2007.
Another story inspired by the tsunami of 2004 and the plight of Owen, the baby hippopotamus who is separated from his mother. Written in third person and stressing Owen's point of view, this book personalizes his loss and later his attachment to a new mother-Mzee, the giant tortoise. See Hatkoff for other versions.

Bernard, Robin. **Insects.** Washington: National Geographic Children's Books, 2001.
A terrific introduction to the world of insects. Packed with striking photos and "Wow" facts, primary kids can't get enough of this book. Comes in Big Book format as well. Available in *The Primary Comprehension Toolkit Trade Pack.*

Butler, John. **Pi-Shu the Little Panda.** Atlanta: Peachtree, 2001.
This simply told narrative will bother young readers. As people chop down more and more bamboo trees, a young panda and its mother lose their home. A great introduction to endangered species and the destruction of natural habitats. Further facts on pandas are included, also.

Calmenson, Stephanie. **May I Pet Your Dog?** New York: Clarion Books, 2007.
This is a "how-to" guide for kids when meeting unfamiliar dogs—a fun way to approach basic safety around dogs. Written in an easy to understand, conversational way.

Cannon, Janell. **Stellaluna.** San Diego: Harcourt Brace, 1993.
Gorgeous authentic illustrations complement the story of a fruit bat who gets separated from her mother. A piece of informational fiction that is great practice for inferring themes.

Carle, Eric. **Animals, Animals.** New York: Puffin, 1989.
Eric Carle's distinctive and colorful collage designs add to the enjoyment of this collection of poetry. A wide variety of writers, styles, and forms are represented—including Shakespeare, Kipling, Prelutsky, as well as Japanese haiku and Native American poems. This celebration of animals is a classic and would be a great addition to any classroom.

Chambers, Catherine. **Tornado—Wild Weather.** Chicago: Heinemann Library, 2002.
Written in easily understood text, this book is packed with striking information about tornadoes with great photographs and visual features about tornadoes, kids explode with questions as they listen to this one. Available in *The Primary Comprehension Toolkit Trade Pack.*

Cherry, Lynne. **The Great Kapok Tree.** New York: Harcourt, 1990.
When a man comes to the rain forest to cut down a huge kapok tree, all of the animals come together to persuade him to save their home. Great book for teaching inferential thinking and synthesizing the big ideas. Available in *The Primary Comprehension Toolkit Trade Pack.*

Cowcher, Helen. **Antarctica.** New York: Farrar, Straus and Giroux, 1991.
A visually stunning story about the relationship between the animals of Antarctica and their endangered continent. Great for teaching inferring. Available in *The Primary Comprehension Toolkit Trade Pack.*

Cowley, Joy. **Chameleon, Chameleon.** New York: Scholastic, 2005.
Vivid, up-close photographs will engage readers. A hungry chameleon searches for food in this tropical rain forest adventure. Text is minimal.

Ehlert, Lois. **Leaf Man.** New York: Harcourt, 2005.
"A leaf man's got to go where the wind blows," and he provides an imaginative journey for young readers. Shapes of leaves become birds, ducks, fish, and other objects in this signature Lois Ehlert piece. Familiar leaves are identified on endpapers, pages are leaf-shaped, illustrations are bold, text is minimal, and the print is large.

Florian, Douglas. **Comets, Stars, the Moon and Mars**. San Diego: Harcourt, 2007.
This beautifully illustrated picture book looks at astronomy through the compelling lens of poetry. Each two-page spread features a short poem and a striking painting about a planet, the sun, the moon etc. The last page has a Galactic Glossary that gives a paragraph of information on the topic of each poem with a list of web sites and resources for further research.

Florian, Douglas. **Insectopedia.** New York: Voyager Books, 2002.
Twenty-one poems and paintings about insects and spiders. As usual, Florian blends science and whimsy with word play and art to captivate young kids. Great for teaching inferring.

Hatkoff, Isabella and Craig. **Owen and Mzee—The True Story of a Remarkable Friendship.** New York: Scholastic, 2006.
"Our most important friends are sometimes those we least expected . . ." This is an amazing account of a 600-pound baby hippo and a 130-year-old giant tortoise, brought together as a result of the disastrous tsunami in December, 2004. Craig Hatkoff and his daughter Isabella were captivated by the story that appeared in the news early in 2005 and joined forces with the general manager of Haller Park in Mombasa to share the adventure with readers. Fabulous photos will captivate all ages. A sequel, **Owen and Mzee: The Language of Friendship,** is also now available.

Heard, Georgia. **Creatures of the Earth, Sea, and Sky.** Honesdale: Boyds Mills, 1992.
Poems about endangered animals and the importance of nature in our lives. Heard's carefully crafted yet accessible poems are wonderful models for children as they learn to write poetry themselves.

Hillman, Ben. **How Big Is It? A Big Book All About Bigness.** New York: Scholastic, 2007.
Readers will appreciate the visuals in this one. "Big" things—such as a python, a tsunami, a polar bear, a pyramid, and an airship—are juxtaposed against "real" photographs—of buildings, football fields, basketball players—to show the relative size of these monstrosities. Text on each subject is brief and will need to be read to younger students; the writing will not be as interesting and intriguing as the photographs.

Jenkins, Steve. **Actual Size.** Boston: Houghton Mifflin, 2004.
All ages will enjoy this "perspective" on selected animals. Jenkins illustrates animals and parts of animals at their actual size. Statistics and further information on each animal are included. Steve Jenkins's **Prehistoric Actual Size** (2005) featuring animals who have lived on earth for millions of years is also available.

Jenkins, Steve. **Dogs and Cats/Cats and Dogs.** New York: Houghton Mifflin, 2007.
This "flip" book format alone will attract readers. To read about dogs, just flip the book over and, vice versa, to read about cats, just flip the book over. Much of the text may require support/explanation from an adult reader. Children will love sidebar illustrations and facts. Younger readers can appreciate the "I wonder . . ." pages on each

animal (why cats purr, chase their tails, and see in the dark; as well as why dogs roll in manure, bury bones, and eat grass!) and the "amazing facts" pages. See his other books, including Looking Down; Big and Little—as art, text, and content are wonderful for this age group.

Jenkins, Steve and Robin Page. *I See a Kookaburra! Discovering Animal Habitats Around the World.* Boston: Houghton Mifflin, 2005.
Husband and wife team up to explore how a number of animals grow and thrive in very different environments. Bold, vivid illustrations will attract younger readers. The setup is "In the desert (tide pool, forest) I see . . ." A map and more extensive information are included at the end of the book. This could be a good way for younger readers to learn animal names and to place them and picture them by habitat. Good format to use as a writing model, too.

Jenkins, Steve. *Biggest, Strongest, Fastest.* Boston: Houghton Mifflin, 1995.
A wonderful book to teach the three concepts in the title through art and text about exotic animals. Great for kids of all ages, readers and non readers alike. Kids can get information from the illustrations alone, more from the simple text at the top of each page, and even more from the paragraph of factual information included on each page. A good example of text with multiple entry points. Available in *The Primary Comprehension Toolkit Trade Pack.*

Johnston, Tony. *Desert Song.* San Francisco: Sierra Club Books for Children, 2000.
A desert night is captured beautifully and poetically. Children will appreciate the language as well as the information in this wonderful read-aloud.

Kramer, Stephen. *Tornado.* Minneapolis: Carolrhoda, 1992.
This author does not disappoint. As much information as one could ever desire about tornadoes coupled with compelling nonfiction writing makes this book a must-have for classroom libraries. A nice companion to *Tornado* in the *Primary Toolkit Trade Book Pack.*

London, Jonathan. *Hurricane.* New York: HarperCollins, 1998.
The power, danger, and excitement of a hurricane come to life in this book set in Puerto Rico. A young boy and his brother swimming in a calm sea notice how the sky and sea change quickly and dramatically and race home to tell the family. A great book any time but especially when studying the weather.

Lesser, Carolyn. *Spots: Counting Creatures from Sky to Sea.* San Diego: Harcourt Brace, 1999.
A great book for primary kids for learning about animals and counting. Award-winning illustrations complement the poetic text.

Lin, Grace and Ranida T. McKneally. *Our Seasons.* Watertown: Charlesbridge, 2006.
Why do I sneeze? Why is there frost on the window? What makes wind? These and other questions are presented "seasonally." Haiku and illustrations will appeal to younger readers.

Markle, Sandra. *Snakes–Biggest! Littlest!* Honesdale: Boyds Mills, 2005.
Snake lovers will be thrilled by the photographs in this book. Nonfiction features include diagrams, labels, map, and glossary.

Martin, Jacqueline Briggs. *Snowflake Bentley.* Boston: Houghton Mifflin, 1998.
The story of Wilson Bentley's determined efforts to photograph and study snowflakes—photographs that are still printed today to illustrate the characteristics and variety of snow crystals. This Caldecott winner teaches kids about what it means to follow one's passion and investigate the wonders of nature.

Milbourne, Anna. *Under the Ground.* London: Usborne Publishing, 2006.
Take a look from "a little way down" past plant roots and animal homes, through man-made additions, past rock, and into the heat of the middle of the earth, and back! The brief information in this text will provoke further thinking and questioning in readers.

Murawski, Darlyne A. **Animal Faces.** New York: Sterling, 2005.
Photographs will capture animal-lovers' attention. Text is simple, yet factual.

Nevius, Carol. **Building with Dad.** Tarrytown: Cavendish, 2006.
Younger readers will be drawn to the design of this simple story. The shape of the book is familiar but needs to be held differently, as pictures and text run top to bottom. Lots of machines are named and simply explained in rhyme as a son watches his father help build his new school.

Posada, Mia. **Robins—Songbirds of Spring.** Minneapolis: Carolrhoda Books, 2004.
Limited, rhyming text describes the life cycle of a robin. Read aloud will be a fun and easy way to pick up some facts.

Prap, Lila. **Why?** La Jolla: Kane/Miller, 2005.
Why do hyenas laugh? Why are zebras striped? Why do crocodiles cry? And why don't snakes have legs? These and more questions about animals are answered both laughably and factually. A fun read for child/adult partners or as a read-aloud. Great for encouraging the strategy of questioning.

Prince, April Jones. **Twenty-One Elephants and Still Standing.** Boston: Houghton Mifflin, 2005.
In May of 1884, P.T. Barnum proves that the newly constructed Brooklyn Bridge can be trusted by lining up twenty-one of his circus elephants across it. (One elephant = 10,000 pounds!) Paintings are striking; this story is a memorable one.

Sayre, April Pulley. **The Bumblebee Queen.** Watertown: Charlesbridge, 2005.
"The bumblebee queen begins the spring below ground and all alone." Thus begins a queen's life journey as she finds a nest, gathers nectar, lays eggs, and tends her colony before the end of the following fall. Illustrations are inviting and accurate.

Simon, Seymour. **Our Solar System.** New York: HarperCollins, updated version–2007.
Science writer Simon teams up with the Smithsonian Institution in this updated version. Fabulous photographs and spacecraft images will fascinate readers and provoke their thinking. Text is narrative and somewhat lengthy. A page or two read aloud might be the way to approach this one.

Swinburne, Stephen. **Safe, Warm, and Snug.** San Diego: Gulliver Books, 1999.
Lovely poems about how each animal species protects its babies from predators. Accurate information presented in a compelling way.

Wheeler, Lisa. **Mammoths on the Move.** New York: Harcourt, 2006.
Written in rhyming verse, this book follows the mammoths' trek south for the winter. Fun read-aloud for young students.

Yolen, Jane. **Count Me a Rhyme—Animal Poems by the Numbers.** Honesdale: Boyds Mills, 2006.
This is the latest work of author Jane Yolen and her son, photographer Jason Stemple. Readers will enjoy a variety of poems and vivid photographs. They've collaborated on other titles with the same format, including **Fine Feathered Friends, Horizons, Least Things** (poems about things small in nature), **Color Me a Rhyme** (nature poems), and **Snow, Snow.**

Science Series

Good books for guided and independent reading, in addition to reading aloud and shared reading

Creative Teaching Press, Inc. offers a number of nonfiction series. The shape of the books are a bit different, illustrations are detailed and bold, and text promotes interaction. Although only 16 pages in length, vocabulary might be tough so teachers may want to read aloud. See **Life Cycles** series (titles include monarch butterflies, fighting fish, horses, and sunflowers), in which readers are asked to put photos in order at the end. In the **How and Why** series—such as **Animals are Poisonous, Spiders Spin Silk, and Plants Eat Insects**—questions provide review at the end. **At the Seashore, In the Park, and Among the Flowers** are a few of the titles in the **Look Once/Look Again** series. Page turning promotes looking from parts to the whole.

Earthworks series, written by David Harrison (Boyds Mills Press) includes such titles as Rivers; Volcanoes; Caves; and Mountains.
These very well done books read as narratives. Language is understandable, art is simple, and the length makes for a good read aloud.

Heinemann Read and Learn published by Heinemann Library.
The size of these paperbacks allows them to be used as read alouds and/or for independent reading. Each chapter begins with a question and promotes interaction; the print is bold throughout; photographs are labeled; and a picture glossary with page references, a quiz, and an index are included at the end. A note to parents and teachers stresses the importance of questioning. There are series about zoo animals, transportation, simple machines, to name a few.

Also by Heinemann Library, see series on **Wild Weather** (blizzards, heat waves, droughts, tornadoes); **Geography** (caves, islands, geysers, glaciers); **Animal Parts**; and a **Dinosaur** series.
These series include more text and a harder vocabulary. Back matter includes a "regular" glossary, "fact file," more books to read, and an index.

Rookie Read-About Health published by Children's Press, Scholastic.
Wide variety of age-appropriate, interesting topics include such titles as **Chickenpox, Sunburn, Bruises, Food Safety, Taking Care of Your Teeth,** and **How Your Lungs Work.** Paperback size is for individual reading. Text is simple yet scientific. Photographs are colorful. Index and "words you know" (with photo clues) included at end.

Rookie Read-About Science published by Children's Press, Scholastic.
Paperbacks for independent use include such topics as matter, electricity, simple machines, sounds, telescope use, the moon, zoo animals, and rainbows—to name a few. Text is simple yet scientific. Colorful photos enhance understanding. Index and vocabulary review (using photo clues) included at end.

Check out the endless nonfiction titles and wide variety of topics from Capstone Press and Picture Window Books.

For your readers who are obsessed with an area, subject, or topic, take time to scan some of the leveled readers series. Seymour Simon's **See More Readers** series (Chronicle Books) offers topics such as bugs and bears, as well as skyscrapers, pyramids, and mummies. Random House's **Step Into Reading** series contains some high interest topics for independent reading. Also, check out **Soundprints' Read and Discover** series which is published in conjunction with the Smithsonian Institution. Publishers are churning out lots of leveled readers. Take time to peruse and decide which are of high quality, appropriate, and of interest to your class.

Science Authors

Some science writers who are of particular interest to primary grade kids:

Janell Cannon	Douglas Florian	Jonathan London
Eric Carle	Gail Gibbons	Anne Rockwell
Helen Cowcher	Tana Hoban	Seymour Simon
Donald Crews	Steve Jenkins	
Lois Ehlert	Stephen Kramer	

Adler, David. *The Babe and I.* San Diego: Harcourt Brace, 1999.
Babe Ruth's hitting streak helps one boy sell lots of newspapers as he tries to help his needy family during the Great Depression. See also book about Lou Gehrig by Adler.

Adler, David. *America's Champion Swimmer—Gertrude Ederle.* San Diego: Harcourt Brace, 2000.
In 1926, Gertrude Ederle swam the English Channel in just over fourteen hours, beating the men's record by two hours AND shattering the myth that women are the weaker sex!

Burleigh, Robert. *Stealing Home—Jackie Robinson: Against the Odds.* New York: Simon and Schuster, 2007.
Main text is one LONG sentence. Each page is beautifully illustrated and also contains a few paragraphs in smaller print about Jackie Robinson's background, the Brooklyn Dodgers, and the prejudice he faced in that era.

Isadora, Rachel. *Luke Goes to Bat.* New York: GP Putnam's Sons, 2005.
A 1950s Brooklyn Dodgers/Jackie Robinson fan is too young to play stickball with the neighborhoods kids. He strikes out when given the chance to play, yet ultimately learns that he cannot give up. This simple story with lovely illustrations makes for a good read-aloud and will provide readers with many connections.

Krull, Kathleen. *Wilma Unlimited.* San Diego: Harcourt Brace, 1996.
Wilma Rudolph overcame childhood polio to become the first woman to win three gold medals in a single Olympics. Her childhood struggles and determination are described in clear language that enables young readers to understand and applaud Wilma's courage and persistence. Excellent model of blending interesting facts with vivid language.

Sports Series

Sleeping Bear Press publishes a series of alphabet and number books. More recent titles include **A is for Axel—An Ice Skating Alphabet; R is for Race— A Stock Car Alphabet;** and **Hat Tricks Count—A Hockey Number Book.**

Highly predictable format allows readers to enjoy the rhyming text and to digest the factual information provided on each page. Topics are of high interest. Readers will appreciate an easy way to gain more information about the sports they love.

Remember to browse through biography series such as **On My Own Biographies** published by Lerner Publishing; **Rookie Biographies** from Scholastic; and **First Biographies** from Capstone Press; as well as leveled readers series. Sports lovers can learn more about "their" sports while learning about the lives of famous athletes.

Bryant, Jen. *Georgia's Bones.* Grand Rapids: Eerdman's Books for Young Readers, 2005.
As a child, shapes in nature please Georgia O'Keefe; as an adult, shapes grab her attention even more so. Eventually, she finds her way to New Mexico, where she delights in all things natural—the sky, the hills, mountains and rivers, animal bones, and the ever-changing colors around her.

de Paola, Tomie. *The Art Lesson.* New York: Putnam, 1989.
This is the story of a young boy who cannot wait to start school and to have real art lessons. Unfortunately, he has to draw what everyone else does. This autobiographical account serves as an important reminder about individual differences. Available in *The Primary Comprehension Toolkit Trade Pack.*

Greenfield, Eloise. *Honey I Love.* New York: HarperCollins, 1978.
A collection of rhythmic poems from around a city neighborhood. Great for snapping fingers, dancing, and choral reading. Available in *The Primary Comprehension Toolkit Trade Book Pack.*

Mayhew, James. *Katie's Sunday Afternoon.* New York: Orchard, 2005.
A playful way to promote interaction with fine art! While visiting an art museum, Katie "climbs" into different paintings and experiences quite an adventure. Five Pointillist paintings are featured. Information on artists (Seurat, Signac, Pissarro) is included.

Micklethwait, Lucy. *Children, A First Art Book.* London: Frances Lincoln, 2006.
Eighteen works of art illustrate activities throughout a child's day. Limited text; stimulating conversation piece to complement a classroom or library collection.

Myers, Walter Dean. *Jazz.* New York: Holiday House, 2006.
Readers (and listeners) cannot help but feel the beat as they enjoy these fifteen poems celebrating the different styles of jazz. Striking, colorful artwork is full of movement, too. Fun for endless interpretations and performances; strong model for writing.

Orgill, Roxane. *If I Only Had a Horn: Young Louis Armstong.* Boston: Houghton Mifflin, 1997.
Based on a true event in the musician's life. Young Louis Armstrong's dream comes true when his neighbors pitch in to buy him a used cornet. A stunning lesson about community.

Raschka, Chris. *Charlie Parker Played Be Bop.* New York: Orchard, 1992.
Great illustrations and words like boomba, bippity, boppity fill this book for primary readers that celebrates the music of the great saxophonist Charlie "Bird" Parker. The rhythmic text is great for sensory imaging.

Sis, Peter. *Play, Mozart, Play!* New York: Greenwillow Books, 2006.
Illustrations are the draw to the book and will make for interesting and imaginative conversation. The very elementary, limited text focuses on Mozart and his father who made him practice all of the time. Readers will delight in Mozart's "play."

Winter, Jeanette. *Diego.* New York: Knopf, 1991.
The story of the famous Mexican muralist Diego Rivera, which speaks to his wonderful art, as well as his love of country. The text is written in Spanish and English.

Art Series

Getting to Know the World's Greatest Artists series is published by Children's Press and is worth checking out. Photographs, artwork, and limited text make these accessible for this age group. See also Heinemann series (Heinemann Library) *The Life and Work of . . .* about famous artists.

Krull, Kathleen and Katherine Hewitt. *Lives of series.* San Diego: Harcourt.
Lives of the Musicians (2002), *Lives of the Artists* (1995) *Lives of the Writers* (1994).
Good for reading aloud to young kids. Great information about famous people from these many artistic walks of life.

Literacy

Banks, Kate. *Max's Words.* New York: Farrar, Straus and Giroux, 2006.
Max's brothers collect stamps and coins, and will not share with him. He decides to collect words—and eventually accumulates enough to tell a story. This is a FUN book for writers (and would-be writers) of all ages, as they observe his process for telling a make-believe story.

Baylor, Byrd. *I'm In Charge of Celebrations.* New York: Simon and Schuster, 1986.
The main character celebrates each day by keeping a notebook of natural occurrences and celebrating each one. A great model for showing children how writers keep notebooks, and for writing short descriptive entries.

Bradby, Marie. *More Than Anything Else.* New York: Orchard, 1995.
Written in the first person, the story concerns nine-year-old Booker T. Washington, who is determined to learn to read. Because he wants to read "more than anything else," Booker will not rest until he finds an adult to help him.

Bunting, Eve. *The Wednesday Surprise.* New York: Clarion, 1989.
In this touching book about teaching, learning, and adult literacy, Anna teaches her grandmother to read, surprising her dad for his birthday and also the reader. Readers will burst with questions and be able to infer the surprise at the end from clues in the text.

Ernst, Lisa Campbell. *Stella Louella's Runaway Book.* New York: Simon and Schuster, 1998.
The most fun read-aloud ever! A must-have for all ages. Yikes! Stella Louella's library book has disappeared and is due at the library by five o'clock. Clever, cumulative tale has lots to offer observant readers.

Heide, Florence Parry and J.D. Gilliland. *The Day of Ahmed's Secret.* New York: Lothrop, Lee and Shepard, 1990.
This story, set in Egypt, shows a very different life for a six-year-old boy than most American children are used to. Ahmed works rather than going to school. But at the end of the day, he reveals his most important secret: he has learned to write his name. Kids wonder about the secret as well as the life of young Ahmed.

Hest, Amy. *Mr. George Baker.* Cambridge, MA: Candlewick, 2004.
Young Harry befriends Mr. George Baker—who is a hundred years old! Both are learning to read, and it is hard. Illustrations add to the charm of this story.

Hopkins, Lee Bennett. *Wonderful Words—Poems About Reading, Writing, Speaking, and Listening.* New York: Simon and Schuster, 2004.
Content and writing of poems make this a must-have. Top-notch poets remind us about the magic and fun of language.

Johnston, Tony. *Amber on the Mountain.* New York: Dial, 1994.
Amber's life high on a mountain has precluded school and reading. A girl moves in nearby, bringing the gift of reading and books to Amber, who returns the gift of a simple mountain life. Kids burst with questions when they read it, and the message that you can do anything you want to if you put your mind to it is a powerful one for children of all ages.

Kroll, Steven. *Patches Lost and Found.* New York: Marshall Cavendish Children's Books, 2005.
The charming story of a girl who loves to draw, but her teacher's assignment to write a story with "words not pictures" causes her much anxiety. Ultimately, her teacher learns something new, as the little girl creates a terrific story in words and pictures. Great book for making connections. Available in *The Primary Comprehension Toolkit Trade Pack.*

Marshall, Rita. *I Hate to Read!* New York: Creative Company, 1993.
A good book to read to early readers, particularly those who are not that thrilled about reading, since Victor hates to read. The characters come to life and lure him into the adventure of reading.

McPhail, David. *Edward and the Pirates.* Boston: Little, Brown, 1997.
Edward, who learned to read in McPhail's earlier *Santa's Book of Names,* now reads everything in sight. One night the pirates come to life in Edward's imagination, and after some harrowing moments he discovers that what they really want is to be read to. A great book for visualizing.

McPhail, David. *Santa's Book of Names.* Boston: Joy Street, 1993.
Edward is in the first grade and is struggling to read. His teacher suggests testing. His wise mom suggests waiting. Edward learns to read when he is ready and has a purpose. This book reminds us that readers learn to read at different times. Great for those children who think they may never read.

Pomerantz, Charlotte. *The Chalk Doll.* New York: Lippincott, 1989.
Rose, sick in bed, gets her mother to tell story after story about growing up in Jamaica. One story leads to another—great model for telling and writing family stories.

Sierra, Judy *Wild About Books.* New York: Knopf, 2004.
Molly McGrew, the librarian, accidentally drives her bookmobile into the zoo. She reads aloud and quickly attracts the attention of the animals, who not only learn to love to read, but also become writers. Written in rhyming verse, this was awarded the EB White Read Aloud Award. Engaging illustrations by Marc Brown.

Whelen, Gloria. *Yatandou.* Chelsea: Sleeping Bear Press, 2007.
Told through the eyes of a young Mali girl, Yatandou, the story tells about the amazing efforts of villagers to buy a machine to grind millet. This will bring needed income to this small African village. Readers come to understand how Yatandou helps her family and community and fulfills her dream of learning to read and write.

Magazines for Kids

A rich array of magazines written exclusively with primary kids in mind.

Magazine	Grade	Focus	Issues	Publisher
National Geographic YOUNG EXPLORER	K–1	*Short articles on science and social studies topics with high quality photos. Classroom sets only.*	7/year	National Geographic Society 800-368-2728 www.nationalgeographic.com
National Geographic EXPLORER	2–3, 4–6	*Short articles on science and social studies topics with high quality photos. Classroom sets in two editions for grades 2–3 (Pioneer) and 4–6 (Pathfinder) contain the same articles at different reading levels.*	7/year	National Geographic Society 800-368-2728 www.nationalgeographic.com
National Geographic LITTLE KIDS	Pre-K–1	*Brings animals, nature, and science alive for the youngest learners. Comes in individual issues.*	6/year	National Geographic Society 800-368-2728 www.nationalgeographic.com
National Geographic KIDS	1–8	*Explores animals, entertainment, science, technology, current events, and cultures from around the world. Comes in individual issues.*	10/year	National Geographic Society 800-368-2728 www.nationalgeographic.com
TIME For Kids	K–1, 2–3	*Weekly magazine at different reading levels for K–1 (the Big Picture Edition, which comes with a poster) and 2–3 (the Newscoop Edition). Also available for grades 4–6 as the World Report Edition.*	30 or 26/ year	Time Inc. 800-777-8600 www.timeforkids.com
Let's Find Out	K	*Language arts, science, and social studies topics.*	8/year	Scholastic, Inc. 800-724-6527 www.teacher.scholastic.com

Scholastic News	1–3	A curriculum-connected current events news weekly. Grade-specific editions come in classroom sets from grades 1 to 5/6.	32/year	Scholastic, Inc. 800-724-6527 www.teacher.scholastic.com
Click	Pre-K–2	Science, exploration, nature, history, technology, and the arts.	9/year	Carus Publishing 800-821-0115 www.cobblestonepub.com
Ask	2–4	Themed issues on arts and science.	9/year	Carus Publishing 800-821-0115 www.cobblestonepub.com
Spider	1–4	Stories, poems, and articles on nature.	12/year	Carus Publishing 800-821-0115 www.cobblestonepub.com
Appleseeds	3–6	Real-life stories about people and places of the past and present. Challenging reading but good teaching content.	9/year	Carus Publishing 800-821-0115 www.cobblestonepub.com
Animal Baby	Pre-K	Simple, illustrated read-alouds about the natural world.	10/year	National Wildlife Federation 800-611-1599 www.nwf.org/magazines
Your Big Backyard	Pre-K–2	Interesting creatures and places of the world.	12/year	National Wildlife Federation 800-611-1599 www.nwf.org/magazines
Ranger Rick	2+	Stories, activities, and articles about exploring and caring for natural wonders.	12/year	National Wildlife Federation 800-611-1599 www.nwf.org/magazines
Studies Weekly	K–3	Grade-specific magazines for social studies (K–6) and science (1–6) come in a national edition and standards-based issues for over 15 states.	24/year	American Legacy Publishing 866-311-8734 www.americanlegacypublishing.com
KNOW	1–3	A science magazine for curious kids explores the worlds of science, technology, engineering, and mathematics.	6/year	Peter Piper Publishing 888-477-5543 www.knowmag.ca
Jack and Jill	2–4	Stories, articles, and activities about science, health, and fitness.	6/year	Children's Better Health Institute 888-257-2530 www.cbhi.org
Kids Discover	3–6	Topical issues focus on social studies and science. Order as a single-copy subscription or by specific edition. Challenging reading but good teaching content.	10/year	Kids Discover 212-677-4457 www.kidsdiscover.com
Weekly Reader	Pre-K–3	Four magazines graded for difficulty address curriculum topics in social studies, language arts, science, health, and career development.	28/year (Pre-K and K) 32/year (1–3)	Weekly Reader Corporation 800-446-3355 www.weeklyreader.com

Exploring Reading Online

These websites contain a wealth of information and activities for students and teachers. The sites in the first section are designed for kids and contain some material suitable for K–2 students. The sites in the second section are designed for teachers or older children but provide valuable resources for the primary grades.

1. Information on these sites is accessible to **K–2 students.**

www.nationalgeographic. com/kids	*Visit this site to explore—in video and text— geographic, scientific, and historical issues and events.*
www.timeforkids.com	*Links in the Teachers section of this site are organized by grade and access downloadable files from past issues. The Kids section provides content for topic research.*
www.nwf.org/kids	*Click on the age-appropriate magazine to arrive at the Kidzone where you will find the National Wildlife Federation's activities and information about animals and animal conservation.*
www.cbhi.org	*Click on the age-appropriate magazine for science- and health-oriented things to read, see, and do from the Children's Better Health Institute.*
www.ocean.com	*Check this out for information—including short videos, photographs, and stories—about marine conservation and the ocean in general.*
www.exploratorium.org	*This website of the San Francisco-based Exploratorium Museum of Science, Art, and Human Perception includes archived webcasts along with other information on a wide range of topics.*
www.classicsforkids.com	*A website dedicated to getting kids interested in classical music.*
www.siforkids.com	Sports Illustrated's *web site for kids.*
www.nasa.gov/education	*The For Students section for K–4 contains age- appropriate information and activities about space.*
www.sandiegozoo.org/kids	*In addition to announcing local zoo events, the San Diego Zoo website offers a wealth of conservation and wildlife information, activities, and projects.*

2. These sites contain resources **for teachers** and valuable information for educators to use with students.

www.inkrethink.blogspot.com	*INK Interesting Nonfiction for Kids This site shares the newest and most interesting nonfiction books for kids. Meet the writers whose words are presenting nonfiction in a whole new way. Discover books that show how nonfiction writers are some of the best storytellers around.*
www.kidsites.com	*A listing of approved sites for kids. The Education category includes links to sites about animals, art, dinosaurs, history, math, music, science, and space.*
www.loc.gov/families/	*The kids-and-families section of the Library of Congress site provides a wealth of information on many topics.*
www.thinkquest.org	*The ThinkQuest library links to over 5,500 free educational websites that were created by and for students.*
www.ecokidsonline.com	*EcoKids is a Canadian environmental education program for youth who care about the planet. The site provides an interactive learning environment for students, their families, and their teachers.*
www.learner.org	*This Annenburg Foundation site, devoted to excellent teaching in America's schools, is organized by grade span. The K–4 section contains information on teaching arts, literature and language, mathematics, and science.*
www.si.edu	*The Kids button on this Smithsonian Institution's website leads you to online resources from all its museums and beyond.*
www.mos.org	*The Boston Museum of Science's student and teacher sections provide great content on a variety of topics.*
www.pbs.org/teachersource	*From PBS, an educator's resource that allows you to search for featured lessons and activities by curriculum area and grade level.*
http://pbskids.org/go	*PBS Kids Go is an umbrella over all the PBS shows aimed at early elementary children, soon to have its own channel on cable TV. Through this website you can access teacher and kids materials built around many wonderful shows including Arthur, Animalia, Word Girl, The Greens, and more.*
www.knowmag.ca	*Features contain interesting and entertaining information and activity ideas.*
www.howstuffworks.com	*A site that explains how things work, with activities and opportunities for exploration.*
www.weeklyreader.com	*A weekly feature and a multitude of resources populate this site.*

Professional Books and Resources to Extend Your Understanding

Allington, Richard L. *What Really Matters for Struggling Readers.* 2nd ed. New York: Allyn and Bacon, 2005.

If you want to learn about best practices in literacy instruction that are supported by research, this book hits the mark. Allington shares compelling research that favors kids spending a lot of time reading books they can and want to read, and covers other areas as well, from comprehension to instruction with struggling readers. But he argues against a narrow interpretation of reading research and he's careful to draw the line when research leads to "blueprints" for instruction.

Alston, Linda. *Why We Teach: Learning, Laughter, Love and the Power to Transform Lives.* New York: Scholastic, 2008.

For teachers and children everywhere, *Why We Teach* offers abundant inspiration, creativity, and hope. Through priceless anecdotes about her kindergarten students—mostly the poorest of inner-city children—Linda Alston shares her wisdom, her openness to children's natural joy and playful spontaneity, and can-do beliefs about herself.

Buhrow, Brad and Anne Upczak Garcia. *Ladybugs, Tornadoes, and Swirling Galaxies: English Language Learners Discover Their World Through Inquiry.* Portland, ME: Stenhouse, 2006.

The authors show how they blend comprehension instruction with English Language Learning best practices to explore inquiry as a literacy pathway for primary-grade English Language Learners. By merging content in science and social studies with thinking in a researcher's workshop, kids discover multiple ways to make meaning. Our *Primary Toolkit DVD-ROM* features the teachers and kids from these classrooms. A must-read for ELL teachers and general teachers as well!

Commins, N. and O. B. Miramontes. *Linguistic Diversity and Teaching.* Mahwah, NJ: Lawrence Erlbaum, 2005.

This book profiles case studies of cultural and linguistic diversity as part of the changing demographics of public schools. The authors provide practical suggestions teachers can use on a daily basis to teach responsively in linguistically-diverse classrooms.

Daniels, Harvey. *Literature Circles: Voice and Choice in Book Clubs and Reading Groups.* 2nd ed. Portland, ME: Stenhouse, 2002.

The quintessential book for teaching kids about book clubs and lit circles. Packed with information for getting started with lit circles, managing lit circles and assessment, the second edition of this classic text leaves no stone unturned. Chapter 8 "Primary Grade Applications" and Chapter 13 "Nonfiction Lit Circles" will be of particular interest to *Primary Toolkit* users.

Duke, Nell and V. Susan Bennett Armistead. *Reading and Writing Informational Text in the Primary Grades: Research-Based Practices* New York: Scholastic, 2003.

The authors make a convincing case for the need for more informational text literacy in primary grades. Emphasizing the research that underlies nonfiction literacy instruction, they share both the theory and practical strategies for teaching with informational text. They show how they teach information literacy through the familiar instructional techniques of reading aloud, shared reading, guided reading, and independent reading. A research article about informational text literacy written by Nell Duke is included on the *Primary Toolkit DVD-ROM*.

Duthie, Christine. *True Stories Nonfiction Literacy in the Primary Classroom.* Portland, ME: Stenhouse, 1996.

A great book for teaching nonfiction literacy in primary grades. The author describes a variety of instructional techniques for teaching nonfiction literacy to our youngest kids, including nonfiction author studies, nonfiction reading aloud, and nonfiction genre study in the reading and writing workshop. Kids love the real world, so the author reminds us to invite them in through nonfiction literacy.

Graves, Donald. *The Energy to Teach*. Portsmouth, NH: Heinemann, 2001.

"Teaching is an emotional roller coaster." So begins Don Graves in *The Energy to Teach*. Even though kids give us energy, the unique demands of the teaching day can sap that energy in a heartbeat. This book describes how highly effective teachers deal with the emotional demands of teaching, how they join together with colleagues for support, and how they cope with the daily "ups and downs" of the teaching profession.

Harvey, Stephanie and Anne Goudvis. *The Comprehension Toolkit: Language and Lessons for Active Literacy Grades 3–6.* Portsmouth, NH: Heinemann, 2005.
The "senior" version of *The Primary Toolkit, The Comprehension Toolkit 3–6* is an extension of the comprehension curriculum that you see in *PTK*. The senior version includes 26 strategy lessons in six strategy books, a CD-ROM, a teacher's guide, a source book of short text, and a book titled *Extend and Investigate*, which includes strategies for science and social studies reading, text book reading, and test reading.

Harvey, Stephanie and Anne Goudvis. *Strategies That Work: Teaching Comprehension for Understanding and Engagement.* 2nd ed. Portland, ME: Stenhouse, 2007.
This practical book stresses the thinking side of reading and features an introductory section on comprehension research, foundation, and theory, a middle section with over forty comprehension strategy lessons, a third section on reading and writing in social studies and science, and a final appendix that includes a variety of short-text bibliographies. All combine to help teachers design explicit comprehension instruction for their students in grades kindergarten through 8.

Harvey, Stephanie. *Nonfiction Matters: Reading, Writing, and Research in Grades 3–8.* Portland, ME: Stenhouse, 1998.
With an emphasis on using comprehension strategies to understand content, this book supports teachers to model the steps in the nonfiction inquiry process and give students time to practice—from choosing topics, to asking questions, to reading for information, to taking notes, to organizing thinking, and finally to writing about and sharing the learning.

Horn, Martha and Mary Ellen Giacobbe. *Talking, Drawing, Writing: Lessons for our Youngest Writers.* Portland, ME: Stenhouse, 2007.
In this book, the authors invite readers to join them in kindergarten classrooms where they listen, watch, and talk with children, then use what they learn to create lessons designed to meet children where they are and lead them into the world of writing. Packed with practical literacy lessons for our youngest learners, this book is a must-have for every primary grade teacher.

Harwayne, Shelley. *Lifetime Guarantees: Toward Ambitious Literacy Teaching.* Portsmouth, NH: Heinemann, 2000.
Shelley Harwayne leaves no stone unturned when it comes to designing a full service literacy teaching and learning curriculum. She bolts out of the starting gate with the importance of books, and moves on to rituals, structures, instruction, teachers as learners, family outreach, struggling readers, and literacy practice for English Language Learners. An amazing book to be dog-eared and coded for years to come.

Harwayne, Shelley. *Look Who's Learning to Read: 50 Fun Ways to Instill a Love of Reading in Young Children.* New York: Scholastic, 2008.
Whether you are a parent, a teacher, a babysitter or a daycare worker, the activities in this book will help you spend joyous moments with the children in your care and support those children as they learn to read and write as naturally as they have been learning to walk and talk. Wonderful for Pre-K and Kindergarten teachers and kids!

Johnston, Peter. *Choice Words: How Our Language Affects Children's Learning.* Portland, ME: Stenhouse, 2004.
Based on research into exemplary teaching, *Choice Words* shares the teaching language that is most closely linked to effective literacy learning. Examples of phrases, questions, and comments are listed in bold print throughout the book. We can easily try out the suggested teaching language with students in our classrooms and trace how this language affects our students' learning.

Keene, Ellin, and Susan Zimmermann. *Mosaic of Thought: The Power of Comprehension Strategy Instruction.* 2nd ed. Portsmouth, NH: Heinemann, 2007.
A seminal book on reading comprehension, *Mosaic of Thought* describes comprehension strategies that proficient readers use to understand text. The authors peel back the layers of their own reading process to give us a window into how proficient adult readers understand what they read. When we understand our own reading process, we are far better able to teach our students to read and comprehend.

Kempton, Susan L. *The Literate Kindergarten: Where Wonder and Discovery Thrive.* Portsmouth, NH: Heinemann, 2007.
In this book, Sue Kempton, a master kindergarten teacher who has spent her career teaching underserved populations, shares the thinking, the structures, and even the precise language she uses to help young children become engaged, motivated, and joyful learners. Sue focuses on teaching her kids to think and she gives her kids time to discover the wonders of the world through books, writing, music, art, drama, artifacts, and even live animals! Sue also recognizes the importance of play in early childhood and stresses how much kids learn and enrich their young lives through creative play. A must-read for kindergarten teachers.

McGregor, Tanny. *Comprehension Connections: Bridges to Strategic Reading.* Portsmouth, NH: Heinemann, 2007.
It's not always that easy to explain abstract comprehension strategies to elementary readers. In this book, the author has created a variety of strategy lessons that make abstract thinking concrete. Tanny knows that if kids can infer, question, and connect outside of text in real life first, they will more effectively transfer these strategies into text reading.

Miller, Debbie. *Reading with Meaning.* Portland, ME: Stenhouse, 2002.
Join veteran first-grade teacher Debbie Miller for a year-long journey through her classroom as she creates a culture of discovery and learning, joy, and respect. Debbie weaves together comprehension strategy lessons, snippets of conferences and guided discussions, kids' endearing responses, and her own practical wisdom. Along the way, she shows us how to listen to and learn from the children we teach.

Perkins, David. *Smart Schools: Better Thinking and Learning for Every Child.* New York: The Free Press, 1992.
Perkins, a professor at Harvard and director of Project Zero there, shares ideas for revitalizing schools. He focuses on ways to bring thinking strategies and dispositions into our teaching and learning and emphasizes how a thoughtful curriculum can motivate kids to engage in active learning. Great book for faculty study groups.

Ritchhart, Ron. *Intellectual Character: What It Is, Why It Matters and How to Get It.* San Francisco: Jossey-Bass, 2002.
A long-time math teacher and now researcher at Harvard's Project Zero, the author shares teaching practices that encourage thinking dispositions such as curiosity and open-mindedness. He discusses thoughtful, practical ways to create a culture of thinking in the classroom and shows us compelling examples of teachers who engage kids in rigorous learning and meaningful discussions. Another great book for study groups.

Routman, Regie. *Reading Essentials.* Portsmouth, NH: Heinemann, 2003.
Full of practical suggestions and research-based strategies for effective reading instruction, *Reading Essentials* illuminates us on four fronts—the essential reading life, the essential reading day, three teaching essentials (comprehension, shared reading, and guided reading), and the essential need for advocacy in the teaching of reading. As always, Regie's practical wisdom gives us much to think about.

Schwarz, Patrick. *From Disability to Possibility: The Power of Inclusive Classrooms.* Portsmouth, NH: Heinemann, 2006.
The title alone says it all. This book presents the idea that "special education is a service not a sentence" and that the inclusion model presents a wonderful opportunity for all of our kids. This gem of a book suggests meaningful, practical, and doable alternatives to traditional school-based special ed practices. The author nudges us to look at

diverse learners, their instruction and support in the classroom from a positive perspective—the possibility of disability rather than the all-too-frequent deficit model.

Stead, Tony. *Is That a Fact? Teaching Nonfiction Writing K–3.* Portland, ME: Stenhouse, 2002.
In this book, Tony Stead makes a convincing case to engage our youngest writers in nonfiction writing. He describes a number of instructional strategies and lessons to hook our kids on the rich world of nonfiction writing. Stead emphasizes that even our youngest kids need a purpose to write and he shares a variety of writing forms such as letters, poetry, interviews, and the like that lend themselves to writing for a purpose.

Zimmermann, Susan, and Chryse Hutchins. *The 7 Keys to Comprehension.* New York: Three Rivers Press, 2003.
At last, a literacy book for parents! Teachers often ask "How do we explain comprehension strategy instruction to parents? It looks so different than it did when we were in school." *7 Keys* answers this perennial question by guiding parents through the reading process and demonstrating and explaining the comprehension strategies their kids will need to be proficient, lifelong readers.

DVDs created by Harvey and Goudvis and of Interest to Primary Grade Teachers

Goudvis, Anne and Stephanie Harvey. *Reading the World: Content Comprehension with Linguistically Diverse Learners.* Portland, ME: Stenhouse, 2005.
In this three-show DVD series, Steph and Anne work together with teachers at Columbine Elementary School in Boulder, Colorado to show how teachers merge comprehension instruction and best practices in English Language Learning to teach kids to think about the content they are learning in science and social studies. Of particular interest to *Primary Toolkit* users is the program titled "Learning and Wondering About Science" which features teacher Brad Buhrow and his first-grade class engaged in an insect study.

Harvey, Stephanie and Anne Goudvis. *Think Nonfiction: Modeling Reading and Research.* Portland, ME: Stenhouse, 2003.
This one-show DVD shows a nonfiction strategy lesson on thinking about and noticing new learning with second graders. Steph models the lesson in a reading workshop and Anne and Barb Smith, their teacher, demonstrate how they work together as partners to read through and talk about the article. Then the kids go out and do the same as the teachers move around the room conferring with pairs. Anne, Steph, and Barb conduct a discussion of the research process in a debrief at the end of the show.

Harvey, Stephanie and Anne Goudvis. *Strategy Instruction in Action.* Portland, ME: Stenhouse, 2001.
This four-show DVD series shows examples of several comprehension strategy lessons in elementary classrooms. Of particular interest to *Primary Toolkit* users are Show 1 "Creating a Culture of Thinking" and Show 2 "Modeling Questioning in a Reading Workshop." Show 1 describes ways to set up a culture of thinking in your classrooms. Show 2 features primary teacher Debbie Miller teaching the questioning strategy to her first grade class. Anne and Steph debrief with Debbie to discuss the lesson at the end of the Show 2.

Pearson, P. David, Stephanie Harvey and Anne Goudvis. *What Every Teacher Should Know about Comprehension Instruction.* Portsmouth, NH: Heinemann, 2005.
Steph and Anne give teachers, administrators, and literacy specialists the chance to listen in as they interview renowned reading researcher and comprehension theorist P. David Pearson to get the inside scoop on the research behind high-quality comprehension instruction. Great for faculty study groups!

Books that Celebrate the Joy of Reading

Burke, Jim. *I Hear America Reading: Why We Read—What We Read.* Portsmouth, NH: Heinemann, 1999.

This book began when high school teacher Jim Burke wrote a letter to the *San Francisco Chronicle* asking readers to write his high school students and share the meaning of reading in their lives. Letters with stories, lessons, and accounts of the power of reading poured in from people across the country. The best are printed here. This book offers a compelling account of the role of reading in the lives of ordinary people.

Fox, Mem. *Reading Magic: Why Reading Aloud to Our Children Will Change Their Lives Forever.* San Diego: Harcourt, 2001.

Best-selling author and literacy specialist, Mem Fox, extols the virtues of reading aloud and describes how bonding through books links not only to better reading, but also to closer, more intimate personal relationships as well. She writes early on, "If parents understood the huge educational benefits and the intense happiness brought on by reading aloud to their children, . . . we could probably wipe out illiteracy in one generation."

Gruwell, Erin. *The Freedom Writers Diary: How a Teacher and 150 Teens Used Writing to Change Themselves and the World Around Them.* New York: Random House, 1999.

As a beginning teacher, Erin Gruwell defied the odds and engaged her "at risk" high schoolers with books and ideas that got them reading, writing, and learning. Four years later, all 150 of her students had graduated from high school, entered college, and become published authors, sharing their stories and lives in this collective "diary." This book is a testimony to the power of determination, high expectations, and thoughtful teaching to transform the lives of kids.

Lamb, Brian. *Booknotes: America's Finest Authors on Reading, Writing, and the Power of Ideas.* New York: Random House, 1998.

For more than a decade, the C-SPAN program, *Booknotes*, has been an oasis of book programming on television. In this account, Brian Lamb, the CEO of C-SPAN, host of the program and writer of a series of *Booknotes* books, has interviewed a broad range of writers about the impact of reading, writing, and thinking on their lives.

MacNeil, Robert. *Wordstruck: A Memoir.* New York: Penguin, 1990.

Robert MacNeil, retired co-anchor of the MacNeil-Lehrer NewsHour, describes an early life steeped in wonderful language and literature. In this sparkling memoir, he attributes his way with words to his early experiences with reading and books.

Pennac, Daniel. *Better Than Life.* Portland, ME: Stenhouse, 1999.

This gem of a book about the joys of reading sold over 300,000 copies when it was first published in France. Now translated into English, it describes how the love of reading begins, how it is sometimes lost, and how to retrieve it.

Quindlen, Anna. *How Reading Changed My Life.* New York: Ballantine Publishing Group, 1998.

The Pulitzer Prize-winning author offers her take on a life filled with books by sharing how much they have meant to her as a writer and a human being. A highlight includes her end-of-book reading lists, such as "Ten Great Book Club Selections" and "Ten Books She Would Save in A Fire." This is one of our all-time favorite books on the joy of reading.

Rabinowitz, Harold and Rob Kaplan. *A Passion for Books: A Book Lover's Treasury of Stories, Essays, Humor, Love and Lists on Collecting, Reading, Borrowing, Lending, Caring for, and Appreciating Books.* New York: Three Rivers Press, 2001.

This collection explores the passion readers have for books, rather than the activity of reading. Filled with anecdotes, essays, and quotes about the joy of reading and written by writers, booksellers, book collectors, and the editors, this is a booklover's dream.

Welty, Eudora. *One Writer's Beginnings.* Cambridge, MA: Harvard University Press, 1984.
Among America's most beloved writers, the late Eudora Welty's literary work has enthralled us for over fifty years. Here she writes about how it all began and shares her early love of reading and the impact that a life of literacy had on her writing.

Wheatley, Margaret. *Turning to One Another: Simple Conversations to Restore Hope to the Future.* San Francisco, CA: Berrett-Koehler Publishers, 2002.
In the spirit of active literacy and *The Comprehension Toolkit*, we include Margaret Wheatley's exploration of the role of conversation in human relationships, organizations, and even world peace. She describes conditions that nurture good conversation and promote real listening. As she says, "The intent of this book is to encourage and support you to begin conversations about things that are important to you and those near you. It has no other purpose." A great read that makes us think again about the importance of "turning to each other and talking!"

Wolf, Maryanne. *Proust and the Squid: The Story and Science of the Reading Brain.* New York: HarperCollins, 2007.
This is the perfect read for anyone interested in the powerful effects of reading on the human brain. Maryanne Wolf shows, through wonderful descriptions of all sorts of readers and her expertise in child development, neuroscience, and linguistics, how "the evolution and development of reading have changed the very arrangement of our brain and our intellectual life." Her synthesis of research and practice gives new meaning to the idea that "reading really does change thinking" (Harvey, 1998).